Beyond Me

Beyond Me

*Poems about Spirit in
Scripture, Psychotherapy, and Life*

CARROLL E. ARKEMA

With a Foreword by Donald R. Ferrell

RESOURCE *Publications* • Eugene, Oregon

BEYOND ME
Poems about Spirit in Scripture, Psychotherapy, and Life

Copyright © 2014 Carroll E. Arkema. All rights reserved. Except for brief quotations in critical publications or reviews, no part of this book may be reproduced in any manner without prior written permission from the publisher. Write: Permissions, Wipf and Stock Publishers, 199 W. 8th Ave., Suite 3, Eugene, OR 97401.

Resource Publications
An Imprint of Wipf and Stock Publishers
199 W. 8th Ave., Suite 3
Eugene, OR 97401

www.wipfandstock.com

ISBN 13: 978-1-62564-538-8

Manufactured in the U.S.A.

"Panic" is reprinted from Springer Publishing's *Journal of Religion and Health*, vol. 49, 2010, pp. 275–76, "Panic," by Carroll E. Arkema, DOI 10.1007/s10943-009-9313-3, with kind permission from Springer Science+Business Media B.V.

"Twelve-Year-Old Face, Holy Heart" is reprinted from Springer Publishing's *Journal of Religion and Health*, vol. 49, 2010, pp. 635–37, "Twelve-Year-Old Face, Holy Heart," by Carroll E. Arkema, DOI 10.1007/s10943-010-9398-8, with kind permission from Springer Science+Business Media B.V.

"God Stammers with Longing, Then Shows Sacrificial Love" is reprinted from Springer Publishing's *Journal of Religion and Health*, vol. 52, Issue 1, 2013, pp. 74–78, "God Stammers with Longing, Then Shows Sacrificial Love," by Carroll E. Arkema, DOI 10.1007/s10943-010-9449-1, with kind permission from Springer Science+Business Media B.V.

Scripture quotations noted The Holy Bible (RSV) are taken from the Revised Standard Version of the Bible, copyright 1952 [2nd edition, 1971] by the Division of Christian Education of the National Council of the Churches of Christ in the United States of America. Used by permission. All rights reserved.

Scripture quotations noted The Holy Bible (NRSV) are taken from the New Revised Standard Version Bible, copyright 1989, Division of Christian Education of the National Council of the Churches of Christ in the United States of America. Used by permission. All rights reserved.

Dedicated to
Roger W. Plantikow,
Friend and Colleague,
who welcomed every poem
with pleasure and affirmation.

Contents

Foreword by Donald R. Ferrell | *xi*
Preface | *xv*
Acknowledgments | *xix*

Panic | 1

Pastoral Formation in the Congregation | 3

Twelve-Year-Old Face, Holy Heart | 6

David, Goliath, and Psychotherapy | 9

Death on the Farm and The Riddle of Samson | 14

Wild Bill Took Down Our Barn, or The End of My Childhood | 29

Crack in the Clock Case | 38

Grandpa Lost an Arm and Wrestled with the Devil, or Was It the Lord? | 41

Uncle Charlie's Funeral | 52

Kingdom of Heaven: Still At Hand? | 57

God Stammers with Longing, Then Shows Sacrificial Love | 74

Something That's Just Mine? or God's Not Even Like That | 79

Broken Ankle, Touched, and Healed | 102

Emptiness | 111

Benjy Suffers Life, and Is There a Point? | 122

Quetzal at El Triunfo | 136

As Her Pastor | 138

Hands | 144

Foreword

It was during my tenure as Editor-in-Chief of the *Journal of Religion and Health* [JORH] that I first became acquainted with Carroll Arkema. As I recall, Carroll wrote me a note telling me that he had recently begun to write poetry as a way of pursuing his own self-healing and as a way of reflecting upon the mystery of human existence. He wondered if the Journal would be interested in receiving his first completed poem as a submission for potential publication. Interestingly, I had just redesigned the format of the JORH. In addition to its predominant focus on the scientific, research-driven, investigation of the positive roles religion and spirituality might play in the enhancement of physical, psychological and spiritual health, I was including a segment in each issue devoted to what I identified as "The Heart Has Its Reasons: The Personal Search for Meaning in Story, Poetry, Prayer and the Arts." I knew this was a bit risky since the *Journal* was not known as a literary or memoir oriented journal. In truth, I was silently calling upon the Divine Spirit to send some copy to support this new Thursday's Child segment of the JORH.

So when I received Carroll's note, I was touched by his own risk-taking. It takes a bit of courage to bring one's poetry to the attention of potential critics, especially as a new poet. In this regard, Carroll's first poem, "Panic," seems well named! However, when I encouraged him to submit his poem for consideration for publication, I soon discovered that we at the *Journal* were not disappointed and his poem was published in the June 2010 edition. When I informed him of our decision to publish his poem, I encouraged him to continue to write poetry and to continue to submit his poetry to the *Journal*.

The book you have before you, reader, is a vivid example of what a little editorial encouragement can lead to! The poems it contains reveal a compelling story of Carroll's individual journey from a childhood deeply shaped by the exigencies of life on a family farm in Iowa to his becoming a caring and effective psychoanalyst/pastoral psychotherapist in the urban fields of New Jersey and New York City. This, Carroll's first volume of poetry, then, is a profoundly personal narrative of the journey of a human soul toward greater theonomous unity with its own depth. It speaks of a soul wounded, yet deeply nurtured by the archetypal world mediated by the biblical tradition and the way that tradition was lived in the kinship community of rural Iowa and beyond. These poems of personal journey are unflinchingly honest and courageous expressions of what I have come to call the "Poetry of Vulnerability." One can learn much about becoming more fully human by reading them.

Yet, the poems in this volume are also subtle interpretations of biblical stories (as well as one on Faulkner's The Sound and the Fury) that seek to express the heart attuned to the larger mystery of good and evil, life and death, toward which these stories point. Here, I believe, Carroll has taken his greatest risk as a poet. In the Post-Shoah, Post Modern world of our time, the poetry of vulnerability resonates in the face of our experience of individual and collective trauma. Such poetry often reflects the loss of the sense of the plausibility of religious and moral foundations that sustain us. It is in this context that Carroll's courageous expression of his own vulnerability may speak to us of our own.

It may be more difficult for some readers, however, to find the same resonance in Carroll's fascinating poetic renderings of the biblical stories themselves. Here Carroll, in contrast to the nihilism of our age, demonstrates a theological confidence that the master narrative of creation and redemption given in the mythos of biblical narrative can still speak to us today in our profound profanity, godlessness and disillusioned secularity. As Carroll sees them, the biblical stories address the human struggle to become, to individuate, to achieve wholeness and a sense of gratitude and relatedness. Thus they speak to us in our brokenness, fear, envy, rage, and terrible suffering; hence, their power and relevance to mediate meaning and healing to our troubled hearts and souls. My fantasy is that Carroll may find himself engaged in much dialogue with his readers over

Foreword

such questions. I surely hope so. In the meantime, we are in his debt for taking the risks that he has in bringing this volume of poems to us as deep expressions of a compassionate heart fully alive in the breath and creative spirit of the Divine. May they be widely read and discussed.

Donald R. Ferrell, PhD
Jungian Psychoanalyst
Editor-in-Chief Emeritus
The Journal of Religion and Health

Preface

Ever since I was a baby, I have heard the Bible read: by my father after every meal, by my mother at time for bed. Scripture feels like part of the fabric of my being, and its stories of the human condition, and of the relationships between God and human beings, resonate deeply with my personal and professional experiences of how people grow, resist growth, and can find deeper meaning, if they choose to, in an acknowledged relationship with God.

Poetry gives expression to all this in a way that's vitally important to me. Much of scripture is poetry, of course, and even much of the prose has a poetic feel or metaphorical meaning which captures and unlocks the mysteries at the heart of existence.

My poems are not light fare, especially the long ones. They're each a substantial meal, and therefore—as when eating satisfying and nutritious meals—it's important to make time and space to get absorbed in them, whether partaking of them by oneself or sharing them with family or friends. Although they're not light reading, I think that the poems have an energy that will carry you through to the end.

I wrote my first poem, "Panic," over the course of five to six months as a less-than-fully-conscious part of my own healing journey. The first line came to me, and the rest began to follow. I felt more and more deeply soothed and satisfied as I worked on the poem. My panic abated, and I could now see my panic in a larger context. I felt that I was a part of something that was much bigger than me. The very writing of the poem, as well as its words, eventually put me in a healing and creative relationship with God—this awesome Presence which is beyond me and beyond any adequate apprehension or description of it. But words and stories about its manifestations remind us of its presence and of our ultimate dependence upon it. That Spirit-Presence is beyond me and within

Preface

me—the very source of my life and breath. But if I don't do my part to nurture this relationship, I increasingly experience darkness, panic, emptiness, void. However, when I'm mindful of my dependence upon that Transcendent Creative Energy or Spirit, I feel more alive, secure, and whole; and I can participate in some measure in that Creative Energy—by partnering with God's healing Spirit in myself and others; by seeking justice; by finding ways of being creative myself—such as writing poetry, doing therapy.

The Journal of Religion and Health published that first poem, which was tremendously encouraging. I've been writing ever since, while continuing to be a Pastoral Psychotherapist and a Marriage and Family Therapist, and while continuing—with satisfaction and resistance—to pursue my own personal, relational, and spiritual growth.

In addition to being therapeutic for me, writing poetry allows me to explore the intricacy and complexity of existence—as captured also in Scripture—and gives me a framework for accessing sometimes detailed memories.

The poem "Death on the Farm and the Riddle of Samson" seeks to capture the remarkable story of Samson's individuation journey—his movement towards becoming a mature intentional person. In the process, he rebels a bit as a way of defining himself in the context of the powerful expectations that his parents have of him and of what he knows about God and God's plan for himself and the Israelites. In the end, when he's stripped of all addictions and pride, he consciously chooses to align himself with God's plan. He surrenders his life to God with far-reaching sacrificial effect, which frees himself and his people from bondage and oppression.

In writing "Kingdom of Heaven, Still at Hand?" I was struck by the relationship between John the Baptist and Jesus. Over the centuries, the focus on Jesus has all but eclipsed the significance for Jesus of John and his ministry. Notice specifically the mutual recognition and respect each has for the other. It became clear to me, as I wrote this poem, that the success and fulfillment of Jesus' ministry is heavily indebted to John's ministry: John's humble ego-sacrificing relationship with Jesus, and also the example John gave

Preface

of speaking divine truth to human power and arrogance—all the way to his death at their hands. He did indeed "prepare the way of the Lord."

As for the poem about Benjy, based on a theatrical performance of sections from The Sound and the Fury by William Faulkner, well, Faulkner, wow, Faulkner! With a seamless artistry that leaves the Reader only noticing it later, he weaves into the novel a contemporary enactment of incarnation: of Transcendent Energy inhabiting someone who becomes a humble but authoritative mediator of a profoundly moving power that pierces to the marrow and leaves one knowing that even in suffering, one is inhabited by Spirit and not alone. I'm referring to the Preacher who—as he gets warmed up—shifts from academic theological language to colloquial African-American vernacular. Again, wow!

I experience and perceive these poems—at their best—as offering glimpses of Transcendent Mystery which is beyond us but also incarnate in human life and in all life on earth. I hope that the Reader resonates with some of what I've written, and catches yet another glimpse of the Mystery inherent in persons and in life and relationships.

Carroll E. Arkema
February 27, 2014

Acknowledgments

I'd like to thank the editors at Wipf and Stock for publishing my book, and to thank specifically Christian Amondson and Matt Wimer for their prompt and detailed support in helping me to prepare and submit the manuscript. Thanks, also, to Springer Publishing for their generous permission to include my poems from the *Journal of Religion and Health* (JORH), and to Curtis Hart, current Editor of the JORH, and Carol Bischoff, at Springer, for guiding and facilitating the Permissions process.

I'm grateful to the patient who gave me permission to publish my poem about our work together, and to all the other important people in my life who have had an impact on me and who appear in—and/or inspire—these poems: especially my parents—Bernard and (the late) Cornelia Arkema—for their spirituality, love, and belief in me; my brothers and sisters-in-law—Dean and Gayle Arkema, and Ken and Pat Arkema—for their excitement and affirmation about having a book published; and the following friends and colleagues: Roger Plantikow, whom I've known for thirty-six years—my first and best supervisor, then mentor, and for the last fifteen years colleague and friend, and to whom this book is dedicated; Charles Mayer and Leslye Noyes for their early encouragement and appreciation of my poetry (Charles was the first to call me a "Poet"); Dan Bottorff, whose long-term friendship and shared Iowa farm origins have led to much laughter and mutual support; Donald Ferrell, who accepted my first poem for publication and encouraged me to send more, which he also published, and who graciously agreed to write the Foreword to this book; Donald Capps, whose writing is inspiring for the way it reveals his fascination with his subject or topic and his pleasure in communicating that fascination to the Reader: one feels his care for the Reader, and I felt it for me personally at his ready affirmation of my website and my work;

Acknowledgments

Jaco Hamman, who showed an appreciation for the best in me from the time we met; Michele Galante, MD, my Homeopathic Physician, whose wisdom, care, and wholistic medicine have enhanced and many times restored my health and wholeness, and who has reflected the beauty in my poetry; and Sal Barrone, an artist friend who eagerly awaited my book.

A special thanks to Mairead Stack, my Life Partner, whose welcoming smile and feisty love and playfulness continue to give me a living experience of an undergirding love which embraces and catalyzes all that an intimate relationship has to offer. In this loving—and therefore safe—embrace, I've learned the transformative power of getting beneath my anger so that I can own, talk about, and suffer/endure the pain and insecurity underneath my anger. Being that vulnerable makes me more lovable and also makes compassion for myself a healing possibility. So what's this got to do with writing poetry? Well, quite a lot. When I'm being with—feeling—my pain and insecurity, I'm less aloof and less defended. I'm being with the whole truth about myself, and I'm therefore open to the light and shadows in myself and other people as I work this all out in any given poem. With Mairead I've felt loved, forgiven, and delighted in—which has helped me do that for myself, for her, and for everyone. Also, her love of literature and the arts has enriched and inspired me.

Most of all, I'm humbled, awed, thrilled, inspired, and upheld by the presence of the Holy Spirit in my life, in my relationships, in my own healing journey, in my healing ministry, and in my writing. I can truly say, "Thanks be to God!"

Panic

Through rolling Time's interstices,
Which I thought neat and tightly sewn,
Sheer Panic pops—or is it Void?—
And rips a ragged hole so large
That Panic's all there is.

Breath won't come, I cannot breathe!
Except for short sharp anxious gasps.
Past and future are no more
The Now is nothing either,
Is death the only out? Please end!

But wait, I live!
I'm not in charge, I need not be,
Of breath and body rhythm.
Unsteady, though.
I search for sense
To make of where I've been.

My life is not my own, I see.
My breath's a gift to me.
It's not for me to make Time flow.
I'm not secure in any Now,
And Void is always nigh.

What Peace I have
Is when I rest
In Source beyond my "I,"
And seek to live in harmony
With Source who lives through me.

The Panic is a wake-up call
To see if I'm on track,
Remembering that I'm not in charge
Of getting born nor back.

I live in Time a little while;
It need not be intact.
I'm held by grace, unending Love;
E'en midst my fears, I can relax.

A man named Enoch "walked with God"
Until, we read, "he was no more
Because God took him."[1] Void's redefined!
As Life with God forevermore.

As Time ticks on now, day by day,
The Void I feared now reminds me
That when I walk and talk with God
I do and do not cease to be.

---

1. The Holy Bible (NRSV), Genesis 5:24.

Pastoral Formation in the Congregation

The Elders are gathered in their Meeting Room,
Eight of the twelve of them.
Sunday worship is due to start soon.
At five minutes till, the Pastor comes in.

As he enters the room, they all rise
In a decades-old greeting tradition.
This Pastor is new here, still ill at ease,
Made more so by this old-fashioned custom.

"Is it me you guys are standing for?" asks he.
"You men don't need to stand up for me."
He graduated in the Eighties from Seminary,
And is more comfortable relating casually.

But he gives off an air of superiority,
A self-centeredness of which he's not aware;
Unable to acknowledge his insecurity,
He compensates with a casual flair.

But almost all of these Elders are farmers,
They're quite used to smelling manure.
A certain amount of it is harmless,
But a big pile of it is hard to ignore.

After weeks of these same protestations,
The discomfort increased on both sides.
The Elders respected his education;
His disrespect of their wisdom was not wise.

They sensed that he was caught up in himself,
That his modesty was actually a disguise
For inner doubts about his spiritual health,
And a willfulness he wouldn't recognize.

Unresolved tension continued to increase;
And everyone began to fear an outburst.
Then one Sunday they heard a still small voice,
Verifying the trope that the last shall be first.[2]

"It's not you that we're rising for, Pastor;
It's for the role that you're sent here to fill."
The Spirit was speaking through Arie Lanser:
The whole room became profoundly still.

The tension immediately disappeared,
But Arie continued to speak;
The Spirit was empowering each word,
Through Arie's voice, which was otherwise weak.

"You're the one who leads us in worship,
You preach the Gospel of our Lord Jesus Christ,
You're set apart and ordained to God's service;
That's the reason—not just for you—we all rise."

Arie was a thin, diminutive man,
Not a man with a big booming voice.
We're often much clearer that the Spirit's at hand
By the irony of the Spirit's human choice.

Wise is suspicion of a charismatic man;
He appeals to the ideal in us all.
We can lose ourselves in his animation,
And forget that the Spirit's in us all.

Pastor's ordination had been self-ordination:
At the center was his ego, not God;
But he was haunted by his own imperfection,
Which he tried hard to deny but could not.

---

2. The Holy Bible, Matthew 19:30; 20:16.

He believed God wanted him to be perfect
Before using him, so he tried hard to hide
His inadequacies, but then all he had left
Was false modesty and a self-deluding pride.

He'd thus set himself up to be desolate,
Cut off from other humans and God.
The real God didn't expect him to be perfect,
But to be humble and empowered by God.

What Arie offered him was the gift of new life:
God's presence as mediated through words,
And a roomful of men channeling love,
Reassuring him he could serve as he was.

So the Pastor was freed from his prison,
Learned the distinction between himself and his role.
He could accept that he was a fellow fallen human,
And that a Leader is servant of all.[3]

The whole tone of that Meeting Room changed:
There was camaraderie and mutual respect.
He learned to welcome their greeting of him,
To receive their blessing like a robe round his neck.

God's Word is indeed a sharp two-edged sword;[4]
But that Word pierces in order to heal.
The cut goes deep to the marrow in the bone,
But then from deep inside out we're made whole.

It was my father who told me this story.
He was an Elder in that meeting room that day.
He was amazed at God speaking through Arie,
And how the Spirit gives the right words to say.[5]

---

3. Op. cit., Luke 22:26.
4. Op. cit., Hebrews 4:12.
5. Op. cit., Luke 12:12.

Twelve-Year-Old Face, Holy Heart

You know how when sitting with someone
Whom you're meeting for the very first time,
Your talk focuses on superficial things,
And at this point everything is fine:

It goes sort of like in a slow dance:
You've gotten together out on the floor,
But at first you don't have much confidence,
That you won't make a stumbling misstep?

But then you get into a good rhythm;
You're learning things about one another,
Of a nature both factual and actual,
Especially about the level of trust.

So it happened one day I was sitting
With a mother whom I had known before;
This time she was there with her daughter,
Poised, twelve, and appealingly demure.

It's June, so I ask about her summer plans.
She tells me she's going to an equine camp
For two weeks with one of her friends;
That she's taking a year off from the other camp
That she attended for five weeks last summer.

With an air of authority she tells me this,
As if she makes decisions like this all of the time.
Next minute she's twelve again, snuggling up to Mom,
A slight wisp of a girl shyly telling me that
She's glad when Mom doesn't have early morning meetings
Because then she, Mom, and their dog Lulu
Can all three walk together to her school.

Then, this is the moment I'm talking about,
In which the person says something which allows
You to look deep into the heart of their being:
You get a glimpse of just who they really are
At their given age and at that moment in time.

She leans forward and says, "Besides,
I'm glad when my Mom is around
Because I mosey."
Her voice dropped an octave or two,
I didn't quite hear her,
So I said, "Pardon?"
Suddenly there was a smile;
Self-recognition shone through her face
As she repeated herself,
With almost embarrassment,
"I mosey, I'm a moseyer."

Sweet, endearing, openly twelve.
Leaving Mom, needing Mom.
Wholly without artifice,
Pre-artifice, an intimate
Glimpse into the heart of herself.

It's our first meeting;
She's felt safe enough to be without charm,
To pull back the veil from her face,
And grace me with
A glimpse of her heart.

We all three chuckle a little;
We all feel full and aglow.
Consciously aware that what just happened
Was a connection we'll remember forever.

Something mysterious and amazing
Goes on behind and through faces:
They mask and conceal but can also reveal
Multiple layers of one person's being.

We read that "the Lord used to speak to Moses
Face to face, as one speaks to a friend."[6]
"Moses didn't know that the skin of his face shone
Because he had been talking with God."[7]

The people were then afraid to come near him.
But Moses reassured them with his voice,
And put a veil on his face until he went in
Before the Lord to speak with Him again.[8]

The power of deep human encounter
Lies in its transparent revelation
Of Divine Presence at the heart of us all,
Which we long for yet can barely sustain.

We approach each other with various rituals,
Share the gift of ourselves in the sacred space,[9]
And in so doing we're transfigured. God is here.[10]
We then leave the most holy place of meeting[11]
And go about our respective daily lives,
Nurtured by the Spirit living within us.[12]

---

6. The Holy Bible (NRSV), Exodus 33:11.
7. Op. cit., 34:29.
8. Op. cit., 34:30–35.
9. Op. cit., Matthew 5:23–24.
10. Op. cit., Luke 9:28–29.
11. Op. cit., Exodus 26:30.
12. Op. cit., I Corinthians 3:16.

David, Goliath, and Psychotherapy

Here's one way that psychotherapy heals:
A patient[13] very carefully helps me see
The subtle nuances of what she reveals
And, teaching me, sees herself more clearly.

Sometimes I just don't get it at first:
The details of what she's explaining to me.
But that is actually not only all right:
It sets the stage for the healing to be.

Before each time she sees her mother,
She is troubled by the ongoing fact
That she inwardly prepares by arming herself
To fend off mother's critical attacks.

Preparing for mother's lobbed missiles
Is actually great progress in fact.
She's come to realize it's her mother who's mean,
Rather than believing she deserves the attack.

It's taken some years to establish this;
To believe that they're not a merged unit,
That she will survive outside mother's orbit,
Even though mother will be importunate.

It's hard for her to believe this isn't selfish
(As her mother continues to aver)
And that accepting her mother's position
Will actually be the living death of her.

---

13. The Patient has given me permission to publish this poem.

But she's taken repeated little risks,
Of standing in her own separate space,
Instead of rebelling and protesting
Which only keeps mother's terms in place.

She's longed to get out of this cage,
To climb off the spinning hamster wheel,
To believe she has a right to her rage,
Which she can use to set herself free.

So I ask "Isn't protection a good thing?
Not be ambushed by mother's attacks?"
She pauses. Then instantly it hits me:
She wants to be with mother relaxed.

She wants to be a little more separate,
And inwardly a little more secure.
She wants to go about her own business,
Not worrying about mother's manure.

Then she makes this most thrilling connection;
Excitement almost lifts her from her seat:
The biblical story of young David,
Who girds for Goliath's defeat.[14]

He took off the armor Saul gave him,
With its weight he couldn't even move.
He went forth as himself, with his staff, sling, and stones,
Empowered by his trust in God's presence and love.

Part of the power of a really good story
Is that each character is one part of us;
King Saul here insists that David wear armor;
Just like my patient, he at first thinks he must.

---

14. The Holy Bible (NRSV), 1 Samuel 17.

But once it's all on, David too takes exception:
He can't move freely with the weight of Saul's gear.
The armor at first seems to offer protection,
But now David sees that it's a mask for his fear.

David in the story is the one who's outside.
He comes on the scene provisions to provide.
He sees armies preparing each day for a battle,
The enemy's psy. ops.[15] is Goliath's proud prattle.

But his strutting on stage is a giant distraction,
Of course neither army really wants to fight.
They're locked in this drama of mutual destruction
Stuck in two options: domination or fright.

Fear plays a big role in the story,
But David isn't caught in its grip;
He dares to imagine the giant can be killed,
But his brother gets angry when he hears of it.

He tears into David with a vengeance,
Accusing him of evil and presumption;
That entertainment's his real reason for attendance,
That even as a shepherd he barely can function.

We begin to see David's resiliency.
He shrugs; says, "What have I done now?
It was only a question."[16] With agility
He turns away and moves on from the blow.

His courage reaches the ears of King Saul,
Who summons him to give an account.
"Let no one's heart fail,"[17] David says,
The Living God's spared me on many a count.

---

15. Abbreviation for "psychological operations."
16. Op.cit., 17:29.
17. Op.cit., 17:32.

Through David, God enters the story;
"The Living God,"[18] David's wont to say—
Implying that in contrast to God's glory,
Without God, it's death that holds sway.

So David takes off all the heavy armor,
Which along with the taunts is pretense;
He's a shepherd with five stones from the wadi,
The Living God is his certain defense.

It's human to believe we're in charge,
That whatever we accomplish is ours.
Through David the story reminds us,
That without God our strength is but dust.

It can be scary to believe in oneself,
Especially without a mother's blessing;
But, as my patient knows, to be anyone else,
Leaves one fearful, angry, feeling "less-than."

David isn't rocked by the giant's deriding.
"You come to me with sword and spear," he said;
"But I come to you in the name . . . of the God . . . you've defied,"[19]
Who today will deliver into my hand your head.

David's move towards the giant is decisive.
The giant mocks him and is proudly derisive.
But David is himself, trusting God, who gives victory:
An instance of God's love conquering fear throughout history.

This Living God "does not save by sword and spear";
 I want everyone assembled to hear, David said;
"This battle is the Lord's,"[20] the victory he'll provide.
The stone pierced Goliath's forehead and Giant Fear died.

---

18. Op. cit., 17:26.
19. Op. cit., 17:45.
20. Op. cit., 17:47.

So my patient is also moving forward,
Trusting more in her own sling and stones.
On new terms which God moves her towards,
She needn't give up her life for all mother's moans.

God's terms are made clear in the story:
Relationship with the Living God is primary.
When that is the core of one's identity,
One can break free of domination and fear.

Like David, one needn't be reactive,
But God-centered, having a plan of one's own;
One can shrug off others' manipulations
If one's self-worth is grounded in God's love.

God will also take care of her mother;
That should never have been her child's job.
Mother's failure to trust God makes her enslave her own daughter,
Whereas freeing us for life is the purpose of God.

So here's another way that psychotherapy heals:
Divine presence is suddenly made manifest
Through an inner connection that the patient reveals;
We connect then in awe and feel wondrously blessed.

Multiple layers of the human mind and psyche
Become transparent and sparkle with light,
Quiet yet palpitating heart and soul energy
Shift and then mend in flashing sparks of insight.

The journey of this patient and the biblical story
Throw light on each other for sure.
We all battle fear, inner and outer harsh voices.
But it's by trusting in God's Life that we're truly secure.

It's a long-term, lifetime-long process,
But giant armies of fear can be routed;
As we trust our simple slingshot resources,
  God's life within us will not be defeated.

Death on the Farm
and The Riddle of Samson

I was probably younger than I can even remember
When I first saw death and whatever was left.
Early on was the smell from the Rendering Truck
As it groaned up the hill of the lane past our house.

Pulling into the yard, the driver jumped down
To ask Mom or Dad what he needed to pick up.
The odor was unique, and lingered for hours;
The truck always reeked with its load of dead animals.

It was usually a hog it had come to collect.
We'd bury a dog, because it was a pet.
It was rarely a cow; they'd leave the farm alive.
I'm not sure where they'd go; rarely sick, they didn't die.

Cows lived quite a while, were valued for their milk.
When their udders went dry, they'd give birth to a calf.
Within hours of birth, the calf was taken from mother,
Put in a pen in the barn and fed milk from a bucket.

Days later it was sold, sucked no milk from its mother.
Cows' milk was like gold; the calves a cute bother.
One thing we learned early from living on the farm:
Protect yourself hurriedly from emotional harm.

My Dad told the story of when he was a boy,
How he'd had a pet pig whom he really adored.
The pig followed him 'round wherever he went . . . .
Then the story ran aground, 'cause we knew how it ended.

Farming is a business, he was implicitly saying;
Getting attached to the pigs will result in much pain.
I didn't realize till later that death was pervasive;
We raised pigs for slaughter and were afraid of diseases.

The death of one's livestock, when it's all about business,
Was the loss of a product, plus work and feed vested.
Pigs easily got sick; I never knew why.
We worked hard to prevent it, but sometimes they'd die.

I remember Dad's panic: our hogs had caught cholera!
He couldn't sleep, was frantic; normal talk became hollering.
Next day the Vet came, very early in the morning;
He had the vaccine. We all would be helping.

I remember we were daunted, because the pigs had gotten big!
With pre-exhaustion we were haunted at having to hold up each
    pig.
We'd stand behind each hog, reach over to grab its front legs,
Lift it up and sit it down, holding it pinned between our legs.

With needle and syringe it got a shot under its arm;
It squealed as if unhinged, too shocked to cause harm.
Five pigs died that summer, out of one-fifty-six.
We'd lose a couple each season; it just went with the business.

II

If the truck didn't come soon, the dead body would bloat;
It would swell up like a balloon, then burst open and rot.
The smell was like a wall one could hardly penetrate;
But a child can't be put off; the unknown would fascinate.

As I ventured in closer, I was scared back by flies,
Who swarmed out in anger, seemed to head for my eyes.
I jumped back in fear; almost ran away;
But then, undeterred, I decided to stay.

All this was new to me: what's with all these flies?
I didn't know then that death nurtured new life.
My next approach was slow, so as not to disturb.
The flies had settled down; a low buzz was heard.

The pig's body had split open: I carefully peeked inside;
I was almost revolted, for a second closed my eyes.
Inside the pig's pink flesh was this writhing black mass,
Atop a wormy white mess, which I later learned were maggots.

Full of awe and revulsion, this was all I could take.
But I've never forgotten the knowledge I gained that day:
What once was alive was not simply dead,
But hosting new life and food for flies instead.

III

All through my childhood, just after we'd climbed in bed,
I looked forward to and loved the Bible stories Mom read.
A favorite was about Samson,[21] the strongest man ever,
Who'd killed a young lion with no weapon whatever.

En route to see his girlfriend, a young lion threatened him,
But "God's Spirit came upon Samson," and he killed it
    bare-handed.[22]
Days later on another visit, he turned aside to see the carcass;
A swarm of bees were inside it, making honey in the lion's corpse.

Samson took honey in his hands, and went on his way eating it;
He gave some to his parents, not telling where he'd gotten it.[23]
As a child, I loved the secrecy, because I too was scared of anger,
Trying to make sense of mystery, navigate a world full of danger.

---

21. The Holy Bible (NRSV), Judges 13–16.
22. Op. cit., Judges 14:5–6.
23. Ibid., 14:8–9.

In a rage at my brothers, I'd slammed a basketball;
It came down on a kitten—my favorite one of all.
It hobbled away, and I assumed it was all right.
We couldn't find it for days. In a window-well it died.

Other deaths I'd observed, but I hadn't been the cause.
I was deeply unnerved; my outburst gave me pause.
I'd killed this little kitten in my impulsive anger.
I'd been afraid of my Dad, now I was a danger.

In a frightening world, both outer and inner,
I was told of God's love, and that I was a sinner.
But those old bible stories reached me more deeply;
About flawed human beings, whom God would love anyway.

That story about Samson was profoundly relieving
In ways I couldn't fathom, but nonetheless healing.
My conscious attention was captured by his rhyme
At his wedding celebration, trying to outwit with his mind.

"Out of the eater came something to eat,
Out of the strong came something sweet."[24]
As a child I was intrigued by the playful irony;
Things ain't what they seem, but inverted can be.

Samson too had discovered that death's a mystery:
What seems like a dead end, may nurture new energy.

IV

The power of this story is that it's seemingly simple;
It isn't clear till later that Samson himself's a riddle.
The riddle and its answer are part of a whole,
And there's layer upon layer as the story unfolds.

---

24. Ibid., 14:10–14.

The answer to the riddle is given as a poem:
"What's sweeter than honey, what's stronger than a lion?"
On the surface it's about a lion upon whom the tables are turned:
The eater is eaten even though frighteningly strong.

From a being that strong, one wouldn't expect sweetness.
Only gradually does it dawn that wholeness holds opposites.
Just so is Samson a bundle of contradictions,
A man of pro-action who will later become a victim.

His wit and his strength are his positive qualities,
But he's also a man with his own vulnerabilities.
All these contradictions, seemingly opposed,
Are part of the fabric, parts of the whole.

The layers of meaning are artfully entwined:
The various themes are there in the rhymes.
The riddle only hints that he's stronger than the lion.
He's still sorting out: "Is this strength really mine?"

An answer still deeper that he'll come to realize later:
A strong man is weaker without the Source his Creator.
His riddle is a metaphor with layers of congruency:
It captures the core of his character and destiny.

He's stronger than the lion and uses his power at will,
But he'll end up being weakened and put to work in the mill.[25]
He seduces the women with his games and his strength,
And in feigning surrender he shows a side that is sweet.

But he betrays who he is in relationships with women;
Trusting only his own wits, he ends up betrayed by them.
The riddle-game he plays seems to be mostly innocent,
It's brains over brawn, but winning's still his intent.

---

25. Ibid., 16:21.

But his wife and her friends refuse to be bested.
He naively assumed they'd accept that he was special.
They outwit him at his game by resorting to deceit,
Turning the tables on him so he's darkly defeated.

Just as the answer to the riddle is divined through deceit,
So the key to Samson's mettle includes betrayal as a theme.

V

What fascinates me next, as it did when I was a boy,
Is this theme about Spirit sprinkled through the story.
His expression of "hot anger" through vindictive killings,
Is prefaced by "the Spirit of the Lord rushing upon him."[26]

How are we to understand this? Is Samson just crazed?
Are we to go and do likewise? Violently rage?
Yet a third time it's written that God's Spirit rushed upon him,
And with the jawbone of an ass he kills one thousand men.[27]

VI

Up to this point in his life, he seems a bit entitled;
Demanding that God give him water so that he won't die.[28]
It must have been difficult for Samson as for us,
To understand what's going on here, to not be nonplussed.

Who here's responsible? Is it God or is it him?
Can he hold God accountable? Or is he on his own?
We imagine Samson wrestling with who he is and why?
What's the nature of his identity and how is he to live?

---

26. Ibid., 14:19.
27. Ibid., 15:14–15.
28. Ibid., 15:18.

If at times God "took him over," how would that feel?
Perhaps he felt grandiose; but what about free will?
His parents must have told him that before he was born,
They'd been visited by an angel and told they'd have a son.

They'd dedicate him to God if his mother would not stay barren.[29]
On the one hand he'd feel special; on the other hand bound.
It's fascinating to read then about Samson's development;
The way things unfolded is complex and compelling.

He knew he was consecrated, a nazirite set apart:
Couldn't drink wine nor strong drink, nor ever cut his hair.
Amidst such restrictions, how could he be his own man?
Would he defy prohibitions, or take a compliant stance?

His parents had expectations, as well as did God.
How he became his own person is what the story's about.
He resisted parental pressure about whom he should marry.
Instead of choosing 'mongst Israelites, he chose a woman from
    Timnah.[30]

In various relationships, Samson's identity is created;
In relation to Spirit, too, he gradually individuated.

VII

This story about Samson is amazing in its own right;
But that it's a story used to tell a story, we must not lose sight.
It's announced in the beginning that God will use this man
To humble the Philistines, who were oppressing the land.[31]

When we read about this dynamic, it's easy to resent it.
If this is the way God would have it, isn't Samson a puppet?
So the story makes us think about what life's all about:
Do we just make the most of it, live for self, then die out?

29. Ibid., 14:1–25.
30. Ibid., 14:1–3.
31. Ibid., 13:5; 14:4.

Or if we're open to God's Spirit and its power in our lives,
Can we then be ourselves without sacrifice?
Do we really have free will, or are we in fact trapped?
Once we're conscious of God's call, can we really turn back?

Let's look again at Samson and how that worked out;
Is there something we can learn from the book of holy writ?

VIII

The back-story of Samson's birth rings out the tone here:
The way the Lord works, turns everything on its ear.
But before we delve into the details about that,
The preface makes it clear that God's behind the action.[32]

God's actions are not bound within ritual constructions.
The fact that they aren't, reveals the relativity of such structures.
In a patriarchal society, the story first mentions the husband;
But the thrilling exigency is that God appears to the woman.

"Although you are barren, you will conceive and bear a son.
He'll begin to deliver Israel from the hands of Philistines."[33]
When the woman tells her husband, he finds it hard to believe.
But the patience of the Lord is something to perceive!

Manoah entreats the Lord, praying that the angel return,
Under the pretense that he teach them what they need to learn.
God listened to Manoah: but appears again to the woman!!
We imagine her smiling as she runs to get her husband.

The woman had told her husband that the man was like an angel;
But he seems not to get it: treats him only from a human angle.
Manoah wants to detain him, in accord with hospitality;
Wants to know his name, perhaps for accountability.

---

32. Ibid., 13:1.
33. Ibid., 13:3, 5.

Seems he can't see Transcendence when looking it in the face;
The angel gives many hints, remaining elusively full of grace.
When asked for his name, he says, "Why? It's too wonderful."[34]
Not seduced by praise: "Worship the Lord," he tells Manoah.

Manoah finally breaks free of his rigid human blindness,
At long last he's able to see that this is a divine appearance.
He directs his thanks to God, to "the One Who works wonders";
And when the angel disappeared, the two fell down in worship.

IX

So the woman bore a son, gave him the name Samson.
We read that he grew, and that the Lord blessed him.[35]
In another part of scripture, we learn more about nazirites:
They're not to go near a corpse, even if immediate family dies.[36]

The locks of their head they must allow to grow long;
For all their days as nazirites, they are holy to the Lord.[37]
There are rules to be followed when consecration is completed:
Offering gifts to the Lord, and shaving the head of the
    consecrated.[38]

An interesting aspect which is surely significant,
Is that the vow is usually taken by one who's an adult.[39]
But Samson is made a nazirite before he's even born;
He has no choice in the matter, it's decided by God.

As part of the preparation, his mother's consecrated too;
She'll no longer be barren, but certain things she must do.
In light of this background, the stories about Samson
Are more amazing indeed, upending ritual and then some!

    34. Ibid., 13:17–18.
    35. Ibid., 13:24.
    36. Op. cit., Numbers 6:6–7.
    37. Ibid., 6:5, 8.
    38. Ibid., 6:13–20.
    39. Ibid., 6:1–12.

From being identified with mother (they're both nazirites),
His individuative journey proceeds in fits and in starts.
In the course of defining himself, he ends up breaking rules.
He separates out thus from mother, but from the Spirit too.

As mentioned before, he chooses whom to marry
Against his parents' wishes; in this goes his own way.
Then this fascinating thing, both intriguing and thrilling:
At a very young age, "the Spirit of the Lord began to stir him."[40]

In a very specific location, he felt something stirring inside;
But he seemed to be alone with this: we read of no human guide.
But the noteworthy thing, as we reread the story
Is that in relation to God, he also finds his own way.

What a wonderful story, the way it progresses:
First the Spirit stirs him, later upon him it rushes.
When the Spirit rushes upon him, he discovers his strength;
But it takes a while for him to discern exactly what this meant.

With the strength the Spirit gives him, he tears the lion apart;
But another reason he keeps it secret is that he's defying God.
Because when the time for being a nazirite has come to an end,
The person offers a burnt offering of one male lamb.

Is Samson turning against God the very strength he's been given,
Is he playing at breaking his vow by killing a lion not a lamb?
Along these same lines, remember what he does next:
Even though he's not supposed to, he goes near the corpse.

He actually even touches it and takes and eats the honey;
And by giving her some of it, he contaminates his mother.
Amidst these blatant breaches, God doesn't cast him off;
In fact empowers and vindicates him when he's betrayed by his
    wife.

---

40. Op. cit., Judges 13:25.

A theme throughout the story is Samson discovering his strength;
At times it takes him over, other times he flaunts it at length.
When he's teasing and taunting, we see another theme come clear:
That of being bound and breaking free, a multilayered metaphor.

Through all of his battles, seductions, and taunts,
He's no doubt sorting out: what's of him, and what's of God?
Those times the Spirit takes him over and he kills so many men,
One imagines that he knows that God is making use of him.

From our vantage point as readers, we can see the whole context:
That at this point in Israel's life, God uses "Judges" to bring justice.
We're troubled by the many killings, and the Spirit's complicity;
But these are human beings suffering oppression; they're bound
    and breaking free.

Death's an ever-present strand in this multilayered story,
Along with how to live, to seek justice, and what to die for.
The writer of scripture through the story of Samson,
Is telling us what direction divinity would lean in.

X

In the overall context of the Spirit being in charge,
Samson moves towards autonomy and making a free choice.
He was a flawed human being, consecrated to God,
Seeking the meaning of the strength with which he'd been
    endowed.

He struggled to break free of the vows he'd been bound with,
Till he threw off the last secret so as to know who he really was.
He tells Delilah he's been a nazirite from the day he was born,
And that if his head were to be shaved, he'd be like any other man.

It's poignant to read that when Delilah shaves his head,
He's asleep in her lap, as though regressed to the womb.
When he awoke from his sleep, thought to shake himself free,
He discovered God had left him and how weak he would be.

The Philistines overpowered him; they gouged out his eyes,
Bound him with bronze shackles, took away his pride.
He lost everything he'd known in his life until then,
And the loss of his eyes left him by himself within.

When forced to grind grain at the mill in the prison,
He experienced bleak helplessness. But his hair grew again.
As a nazirite from birth, God through mother had claimed him.
Now that he'd broken his vow, he was truly a free man.

XI

Free though imprisoned, blind beginning to see,
Broken addiction to women: what's central to me?
My strength, yes, my strength, but now it's clear to me
That my strength leads to nothing if it's all about me.

My relationship with God—being allied with God's cause—
Is what can give my life meaning, not just me for myself.
For years I've gamed helplessness, being bound then breaking free;
Now that I'm really helpless, is there a way out for me?

A major thrust of my whole life has been defining myself and
Becoming responsible for my energy, seeking freedom from
    oppression.
Though blind I now see: God wants the same things;
I'll only be truly free if I'm allied with him.

XII

One thing about Samson is that he never lost hope;
Since he'd been threatened by the lion, he'd found strength to cope.
He clearly knew now that his strength's source was the Lord;
So now, for the first time, he initiates contact with God.

At the Philistines' celebration to rejoice at his capture,
Thanking their god for giving them their ravager,[41]
They bring him from prison, demand that he entertain them.
He doesn't accept humiliation; Samson's devising a plan.

Near the end of the story, several themes come full circle;
There's continuing irony, and some satisfying reversals.
The one who'd been deceived by his wife and betrayed,
Will now make use of deceit his strength to display.

He gets himself positioned between the house's central pillars,
Fully aware of his condition, that without God he's powerless.
Having bridled for so long at being chosen by God and bound,
He now freely chooses God from the autonomy he's found.

He calls out to God in a respectful reverent prayer,
"Strengthen me just this once that this wrong I may repair."[42]
He wants revenge for himself for the loss of his eyes;
But it's no longer for ego, because he knows that he'll die.

It can't have been lost on him that God wants justice too,
So he offers himself as a sacrifice, thus completing his vow.
Thus just as the lion's death was redeemed by the honey,
His choice sweetens God's cause, since he has to die anyway.

He's now become his own man, getting revenge for himself;
While also being God's man by his own considered choice.
He leaned against the pillars, and brought the house down,
As he poignantly prayed, "Let me die with the Philistines."[43]

---

41. Ibid., 16:24.
42. Ibid., 16:28.
43. Ibid., 16:30.

XIII

All the killing seems excessive; can this be God's will?
What sense can we make of this? Because it's happening still.
Perhaps it's driven by pride, as in Samson's life journey;
But at the spiritual level, we can fulfill God's will differently.

Hosea[44] reveals God's heart, recoiling within,
Which though betrayed, renounces wrath, is tender and warm.[45]
These people! God cannot forget having lovingly raised them,
This unfaithful people, God just cannot destroy them.[46]

This God of love rages, but chooses not to be violent,
Instead calls to the people and to a better life invites them.[47]
Perhaps Samson's way of dying, of sacrificing his ego,
Hints at a new paradigm, which people didn't yet know.

He takes violence into himself in the service of justice,
Without domination, and moving towards "God with us."
In this story of Samson, we can see our own selves,
Created to do God's will, but free to choose how we live.

In the course of self-discovery, we'll go our own way,
Betraying God, self, and others as we form an identity.
Most of us break some rules, but that can help us see
Why the rule was even there; and we discover humility.

God supports us in our journey from merger to autonomy,
Delighting in our uniqueness, from a distance or intimately.
God's with us throughout our journey in every breath we breathe,
Calling us to be aware of that, and showing us how to live.

---

44. Op. cit., Hosea 11.
45. Ibid., 11:8b.
46. Ibid., 11:9a.
47. Ibid.,, 14;1–9.

In the story about Samson, things aren't what they seem.
The Spirit is ever present, and life's full of mystery.
We're influenced by strong forces which may take us over,
And coming to terms with these forces, will determine who we
    are.

XIV

Many things about this story, as a child on the farm,
Resonated at many levels, as I'm continuing to learn.
Just as death was omnipresent, though most of the time latent,
So these themes were all present, and only now more explicit.

I found it comforting then, and encouraging still
That God's presence gives life meaning, and also death as well.
Already as a little child, death was smelly and scary,
But even then as well, it was a portal to mystery.

Already way back then, through my own mother too,
God was made known to me, and I'm so grateful now.
The external visible life of an extraordinary man
Was just part of the fabric of the invisible Spirit in him.

A final moving touch to this most amazing story
Is that where God first stirred him is where he was buried.
"The Spirit of the Lord began to stir him between Zorah and
    Eshtaol."[48]
"His brothers and all his family . . . buried him between Zorah and
    Eshtaol."[49]

We're born, we live and die: it all comes full circle.
There's always more life, and it's all such a miracle.

---

48. Op. cit., Judges 13:25.
49. Ibid., 16:31a.

Wild Bill Took Down Our Barn, or The End of My Childhood

Thirty-five feet in the air,
Sitting astride the peak beam,
Supported now only by
The few remaining rafter beams,

He was hammering out the pegs,
Which were the only thing left
Locking those rafters
To the beam upon which he sat.

The peak beam itself was in two parts,
Held together by two pegs in the middle
Through the mortise and tenon
Interlock of those ten-inch square beams.

In his narrow-brimmed round hat
And wild red plaid coat,
He was edging backwards
As he banged out the pegs
And the rafters came crashing down.

It scared me and thrilled me
To see him up there;
I envied him and hated him
For taking down our barn.

I was twelve or thirteen;
That barn was my life.
Built in mid-nineteenth century Iowa
It had survived until now nineteen sixty.

I felt safer there by far
Than I'd ever felt in our house.
Somehow the brute power, need,
And sex lives of the animals
Felt more manageable than
The outbursts of anger from my father.

We entered the straw-covered dirt floor of the barn lobby
Through two wide sliding doors on rails.
Pitchforks, shovels, scythes: various tools hung on the lobby walls
Between doors to the granary bins on one side,
The door to the feed-trough for the cows
Behind their stanchions on the other side,
And the door at the far end to the back of the barn.
The wall-ladder to the loft
Was on the rear left side of the lobby.
I'd jumped down several times
From the loft to the floor of the lobby,
Though much less often after I'd once
Banged my chin on my knee upon landing
And could have bitten off my tongue.

The loft was a world unto itself
Full of mystery, fear, fun and dust motes:
Three large sections divided by beams and uprights,
Loose hay on one end, baled straw in the middle,
Baled hay on the other end.
Up under the peak beam hung an iron pulley track
Which extended out through the huge gable door
To the end of the extended roof overhang,
So that a rope from the pulley could drop down outside
To the ground or to a wagon to pull up hay or straw
Into the barn in the old days, before elevators.

So hot as to be almost unbearable in Summer,
The loft was cold though somehow cozy in Winter.
It was a danger-filled thrill
To climb the beams and bales

And dare each other to jump;
To balance oneself walking the higher beams,
hoping not to fall;
Or to play almost hopeless hide and seek.

Back on the ground level of the barn,
The rear lobby door led back
To the animal areas of the barn.
Straight beyond that rear lobby door
Was the large back door to the outdoors
Through which the cows entered the barn
Morning and evening to be milked.

Each of the sixteen cows knew its place,
And would march with careful alacrity
To its designated stanchion, put its head through,
And begin eating the enriched ground corn meal
In the trough while my Dad or I
Followed them and closed the stanchions.

My Dad would then proceed to install
The three electrical milking machines
In regular rotation till all cows were milked.
Things usually went without a hitch, unless
A young cow was being milked for the first time,
Or some other cow was in a devilish mood.

The "first-time" cow would tense up and dance around,
Wondering why some human was touching her udder
And then not be at all inclined to cooperate
With a milking machine being attached to its teats.
There was a definite art to handling a cow,
And my Dad was as good or better at it than anyone.

It would begin with a soothing voice
As he approached from the rear alongside the cow,
Placing a calm hand upon its back,
Trying to manage his own terror

Of the cow possibly delivering a powerful kick
Or hopping around and stepping on my Dad's foot.

All this while holding the milking machine
In his other hand, and being between
The adjacent cow and the one he was training.
As if that's not scary enough,
Then in that vulnerable position
Having to courageously bend down
To attach the milking machine's suction cups
To the terrified cow's four teats!

Some cows were more receptive than others,
And there was the option of hobbling or tying
The cow's rear legs so it could neither kick
My Dad, nor kick off the milking machine.
In the worst cases, the art of milking expanded
To include lots of cursing, name-calling,
And twisting of the cow's tail into unimaginable positions
In an effort to dominate and force the cow to cooperate.

Which she eventually did,
Though with an occasional surprise kick,
Perhaps just to assert
That she still had that option.
That led again to lots of cursing and retribution,
And some cows just always had to be hobbled.

There was always the threat, too,
Of a cow suddenly shitting or pissing
While stanchioned in the barn.
There was a gutter running along the floor
Behind the cows for this purpose,
But it was usually inadequate to handle
The force of nature's excretory power,
So one needed to jump clear at any moment
In order to avoid getting splattered.

My daily chores included putting the enriched grain
Into the trough with a measuring can;
Carrying the milk in a five-gallon bucket
In all kinds of weather to the tank in the milk shed
Some fifty yards away from the barn
Without spilling a drop, let alone dropping the bucket,
Under dread of severe punishment;
And cleaning the manure out of the gutters
By heaving it with a shovel out the barn windows.

On the farm, and in this part of the barn,
There was shit everywhere:
On the floor of the barn, on the walls of the barn,
Piles of it outside the barn;
But shit and the smell of it was part of farm life,
The dried variety highly preferable to the fresh wet.
Clean straw helped considerably to absorb the muck
And made a remarkably warm bed for the cows in winter.

Once on that straw I remember a cow moaned in agony
As it tried to deliver a breach-birth calf.
My Dad had gotten it into the barn,
Stanchioned as if to be milked,
And I watched in disgust and bloody awe
As my Dad and the Vet pushed the emerging calf
Somehow back into the cow and turned it around
So that the cow could give it a normal birth.
That time, all ended well.

All this took place on the right and back side of the barn.
To the left and back side of the barn
Were two or three overflow stanchions,
And two pens: one for the newborn calves
And one—with thick plank walls—for the bull.

Most of the time we didn't have a bull.
He was too much trouble.
Once let out of the pen to mate with a cow,

It would be hard to corral him
And get him back into the pen.
Besides, being penned up most of the time
With no exercise, was unhealthy for the bull.
But if he were allowed to roam freely with the cows,
He'd break fences and wander the neighborhood.
Most of the time, therefore, the cows
Were artificially inseminated.
Whenever a cow was in estrus, in heat,
She was kept in the barn in a stanchion,
And the Artificial Inseminator was called.
He'd show up, enter the barn with the cow,
Roll up his left shirt sleeve,
Lubricate his whole left hand and arm,
Gradually shove it all the way into the cow's vagina,
Then insert a long narrow tube filled with bull semen
Alongside his arm and inject the semen into the cow.

Nine months later the cow had a calf.
The calf would be taken from its mother,
Put in the pen, and fed milk from a bucket
Which had an artificial teat.
The cow was then milked morning and evening
For six or seven months, till its udder dried up.
Then the cycle was repeated.

All this in that barn during my early years:
Where my two brothers and I would play on rainy days,
Where I was introduced to and participated in
These elemental rhythms of animal and human life.

I felt a strangely safe yet awe-filled connection
To ancient and primitive rituals
Involving man and beast and survival,
Which were certainly bigger than me,
But in which I could also participate.

My Dad built wagons in the lobby of that barn;
We put up hay and straw in the loft of that barn;
We ground corn—cob, kernels, and all—
Into the granaries of that barn;
We saw newborn kittens in the manger of that barn.
My brothers and I played with matches,
And smoked our first cigarettes, in the straw of that barn!
It's a wonder it survived, that we didn't burn it down.

My Dad shot and killed one of our dogs in the barn
In order to euthanize it after it had sustained
Internal injuries from being grabbed
On the top of its back and shaken like a dog shakes a rat
By the huge angry mouth of a farrowing sow
Who thought the dog was a threat to its newborn piglets.
The dog had innocently followed me into the pigpen,
Which I'd entered in order to feed the sows.
This shocking new thing had happened in a flash.
I'd never seen, known, nor heard of a hog doing such a thing.
The dog did get away and dragged itself to the barn.
I finished feeding the pigs, but was badly shaken myself
    emotionally
By the ferocious maternal protectiveness of that sow.
I was relieved that the dog had gotten away,
Until I saw it the next morning lying dead still in the barn lobby
With a bloody hole in the top of its head.

When I asked my Dad what had happened,
He told me he'd had to shoot it early that morning
Because it had been howling in pain all night
From internal injuries. I felt dumb and numb
With shock and guilt and loss, and rage at my Dad.
The death of animals was an ever present danger on the farm.
Hell, we raised animals to be butchered for food!
But not a pet dog; and for him to kill the dog!

I was confused, too, because he had happily brought the dog home
As a pup a few months earlier, and he'd seemed to like the dog.
But I wouldn't have wanted the dog to suffer either,
And the sow was just protecting its pigs. . . .
I was struggling to put it all together,
Especially the image of him taking up the gun,
Approaching the dog, and then pulling the trigger.
He'd spanked me hard at times, but how scary was he?

All this, and more, in that barn
Which Wild Bill, astride now its naked beam,
Was dismantling.
I remember exactly where I was standing:
Beside the Machine Shed, watching him.

This was probably the fifth day
He'd been there. On previous days
I'd come home from school and seen
The results of his labors.
The weathered red siding boards
Had already been ripped off, along with
The thin strips of ship-lap which had covered
The cracks between the boards.

The hay and straw had all been removed,
Along with the shingles and sheathing of the roof.
The guts of the barn had been pulled out,
Taken apart, and discarded or burned.
The stanchions; the boards
Which had formed granaries or pens;
The walls of the lobby; the logs laid
Side by side to form the floor of the loft;
The doors, the windows, all gone.

Only Wild Bill was left, high astride
Those huge, adze-hewn timbers
Which formed the frame of the barn:
Like the skeleton which remains
When all tissues have been removed.

Seeing Wild Bill framed up there in the sky
Was the last thing I remember
Before the barn was no more.
How he got that last beam down
Upon which he was sitting,
I do not know.
I either had to go do chores
Somewhere else on the farm,
Or I just couldn't bear to watch
To the end.

That everlasting image
Of Bill astride that peak timber:
Taking down our barn,
Was the end, I see now, of my childhood.

The dismantling of that old barn
Prior to replacement with a new one,
Was more powerful, in many ways,
Than a Bar Mitzvah or Confirmation,
With Wild Bill representing a rabbi or priest
Marking my rite of passage
From boyhood into nascent manhood.

Crack in the Clock Case

Dad made this Grandfather clock—
    Its walnut case, that is—
    His first.
He didn't make the works—
    The part that ticks
    And tells time.

He'd buy and install the works,
    No easy task
    In its own right:
The scaffolding for the works
    Inside the clock
    Had to be just so,
Or the axle for the hands
    Wouldn't fit through
    The tiny hole
Of the decorated gold metal face
    Facing front, which you see
    When you look at the clock.

This first clock he made
    Was for my youngest
    Brother Ken,
As a gift for his wedding
    At the young age
    Of eighteen.

But the point of this poem,
    Lest I go on
    Too long,
Is that one day while visiting
    At Ken's home
    With my parents,

During a lapse in conversation,
    I noticed my Dad looking
    At Ken's clock.

He stepped up closer to it
    And edged a sheet of paper
    Into a crack,
Which shouldn't have been there
    If the 45-degree angles
    Had fit tightly together.

He showed no visible regret,
    But he couldn't help but check
    His handiwork;
The way a master craftsman does
    With his earlier work
    Which is less perfect.
It was good enough at the time,
    Maybe the best he could do,
    But he has since moved on.

Such is the way with our selves:
    We could do with reflecting
    On our slight imperfections.
We can wish the crack wasn't there,
    But it makes us aware
    We're a work in progress.

We needn't seriously regret
    What cracks we see,
    But look honestly,
Realizing that who we were
    At any given point in time
    Is always imperfect.

The Divine Master Craftsman
    Through the Spirit lodged in us
    Keeps molding us,

Believing that the next manifestation
    Will more accurately accord
    With the image of the Lord.

Grandpa Lost an Arm and Wrestled with the Devil, or Was It the Lord?

Unfortunately for him, this wasn't
One of the countless near misses
Which always leaves us breathless
With what a scary-close brush
We've had with disaster.
Nor was it a nightmare.

Worse. This time for him disaster lay
In wait on an ordinary work day:
He was walking slowly alongside
The huge trench-digging machine
That he was guiding and operating,
With gloves on; a chilly autumn day.

The machine was moving along apace,
Its motor roaring full throttle,
Its Ferris wheel of cutters
Heaving dirt from the ground,
Leaving behind a five-foot deep trench
Into which five-inch drainage tile were laid.

He'd done this work for years now,
Loved the efficiency of the machine,
Which made it possible to drain
The sloughs so as to make available
More land for farmers to till:
The water ran underground now.

Occasionally the engine would groan
When the cutters hit a rock
Or a buried root or a creeked antique.
But usually it groaned and moved on.
It took a lot to stop the roar
Of an engine with all its power.

Exposed on the side of the machine,
A rapidly spinning drive shaft—
With two sets of universal joints
Which enabled the shaft to turn corners—
Carried power from the engine
To the wheels and to the rear cutting wheel.

This was the period before
Thorough safety regulations;
Before protective shields
Or steel guards were in place.
Nowadays the manufacturer
Would be sued for what happened.

Something fell onto the drive shaft—
A piece of root, a clod of dirt, a stone.
As he'd done so many times before,
Grandpa reached over to brush it off.
The tip of the glove on his right hand
Got caught in the universal joint,

Which in its rapid rotation wound
His hand and arm around
The shaft up to his elbow,
Crunching bones and flesh and rolling
Them up like paper so fast
That it was over before he knew
That his elbow had stopped the engine.

In shock over what had happened,
Grandpa somehow unwound his mangled arm,
Walked several hundred yards to his pickup truck,

And drove the couple miles to our farm.
He found my Dad—we kids were in school—
And asked him to cut off his arm

With a pocketknife. The arm was dangling—
Attached only by a section of skin.
My Dad did as he was asked, vomiting,
Then drove him to the hospital.
I've always wondered what they did
With the arm. Never dared to ask.

My Dad never talked to me about it.
I was about eleven at the time.
I loved my grandfather. He and Grandma
Lived in town, a couple miles away.
My parents, two brothers, and I
Went to their house every other Sunday.

We and the families of three other
Aunts and uncles would go there
After the Sunday evening worship service
For coffee, juice, homemade desserts.
But even more importantly, to converse;
And for me, after age thirteen, to listen.

Those were sacred times for me.
Grandpa himself—when I turned thirteen—
Invited me to sit in the parlor with the men.
The women would gather in the kitchen,
Where they prepared the food and "visited."
This was two years after the accident.

It was there, sitting with those men,
That I heard the details from Grandpa
About what had happened.
He was still coming to terms
With the trauma of losing his arm.
He wore a primitive prosthetic hook.

All of us were raptly listening.
He was a wonderful storyteller
Anyway, but this was gripping.
While slowly shaking his head,
He spoke of wrestling with the devil
About it all in the middle of the night.

"The absence of my arm was terrifying,
I'd awaken, try to prop myself up, roll over,
And there was nothing there!
Not to mention that it hurt like the devil
For a long time. And all my own fault.
Though somehow, I felt angry with God, too.

Anyhow, I sure talked to God about it.
But He didn't touch it and restore it,
Like Jesus did with Malchus' ear[50].
Night after night, the devil would appear,
Rubbing salt into my wound and shame.
Everywhere I'd go, I'd never be the same.

If only I'd been a little more careful;
I'd done that a hundred times before,
I definitely should have known
better than to do it with gloves on.
I wanted to believe it hadn't happened.
If only I could go back, and do it over again.

Everyone now would know I was stupid.
Mortally ashamed, I just wanted to hide.
The devil made a good case for suicide:
To slip out of bed in the middle of the night
And end it all with a goddamn pocketknife!
O, looking back, I can see it was Pride.

But you know, it was my body!
My right arm was part of my body!

    50. The Holy Bible (NRSV), Luke 22:47-53; John 18:1-11.

For the longest time I couldn't believe it was gone.
The doctor talked about dealing with the phantom
Limb: that I would think it was there but it wasn't.
But the more powerful phantom was Satan.

The devil was as real as me in the dark of night.
I haven't met a doctor yet who could understand that!
But you know, boys, what I thought was the devil and me,
Was actually me putting myself up against God,
The more I'd blame myself for what happened,
Or get angry with God for the final movement of that hand,

I came to realize that I was only fighting and not accepting
That I was now just in this world in a whole different way.
Having that arm was a way I related to everything;
Now I couldn't even use it the way I'd learned to pray!
It was humbling to realize I was fighting with God, not Satan;
Not accepting my wound, I wanted to be sovereign.

O, that story of Jacob wrestling with the angel[51]
Came to me one night, and gave me a different angle
From which to look at all this. He plotted
With his mother, deceived his father and brother
To get his own way, and they even succeeded;
Though he had to leave her and run away to his uncle.[52]

His loss was different than mine. He lost his home,
Was a fugitive for a while; thought he was alone,
Had a dream of God's presence while asleep on a stone.[53]
He went on with his journey, left his past behind,
But God's angel caught up with him upon his return.
And gave him one more opportunity to learn.

He couldn't run away from himself, from what he had done,
Nor get around meeting his brother Esau on his way home.

51. Op. cit., Genesis 32:22-32; context is Genesis 25:19—33:20.
52. Loc. cit., 27:1— 28:9.
53. Ibid., 28:10-22.

Jacob had been visited by God in that fugitive dream,[54]
But he'd continued to succeed by being cunning.
He got things all backwards about who was in charge,
Mistook God's presence as blessing while Jacob dealt the cards.

He was scared of his brother, and expected revenge,
Tried to appease him with goods, and thus make amends.[55]
Still thought it was up to him—that he was in control;
Just plotted more desperately than he ever had before.
But when it began to look doubtful that this time he'd win,
He couldn't sleep that night, crossed the stream to look within.

Wrestled all night with an angel, we read in The Book.[56]
Jacob's energy was so strong that he almost overtook
The angel, who was the Spirit of God in Jacob.
Jacob's power was such that he had the angel pinned,
Until the angel begged Jacob to let go of him.
Jacob said, 'I'll not let you go unless you bless me.'

Now you see, men," Grandpa was teaching, I hardly breathing,
"Jacob's now begging for a blessing, which earlier he stole
Through deceit from his brother. He and the angel begging
Each other for what each and every one of us needs to be whole:
Freedom and blessing: freedom to be our separate selves,
Blessing to know that it's okay—necessary for our growth.

Both so vulnerable that they couldn't be more intimate:
Skin on skin, sweat mixing with sweat—like I've sweat
Wrestling with my angel—locked in desperate combat
Over who's in ultimate control. This time Jacob gets it.
Up till now, didn't feel a man unless he was in control.
Now knows that Spiritual power means being vulnerable.

Do you hear this, men, hear what's hidden in this story?
We talk about almighty God: there's nothing he can't do.

54. Ibid.
55. Ibid.., 32:3–21.
56. Ibid., 32:24.

In terms of who's ultimately in control, that's true.
But what I see now about how God relates to you and me
Is that God does not give life or show love forcibly,
But engages us, relates to us, in vulnerability.

We try to control another's spirit, seeking security;
But that restricts the other's power, because he's not free.
Which results in stalemate, deadlock in dark of night.
Grandiose delusions of control that won't survive in daylight.
As day dawns, Jacob begins to see that his power's not his own.
And he realizes now that without God he'll always be alone.

The angel knows that as day dawns, he cannot be seen;
This nighttime wrestling is a drama that happens within,
But it's no less real for being what we call a dream.
It's so real in fact that Jacob emerges walking with a limp:
Because when the angel realized that he would not prevail,
He played his trump card while remaining vulnerable.

He struck Jacob on the hip and put it out of joint—
Or perhaps in anguish Jacob stumbled and fell;
But however it humanly happened, the point
Is that the Spirit of God in Jacob would prevail.
'But if I'm not in charge, and now you've crippled me,
I'm afraid to let you go unless you bless me being me.'

The Spirit knows of course that Jacob's pride is hurt,
That his characteristic way of being is falling apart.
As the second-born of twins, he'd refused to accept his lot;
Esau was their father's favorite: would inherit all father'd got.
So Jacob became a deceiver, stole his brother's birthright;[57]
Later also out-witted his uncle, but paid a hefty price.

Uncle Laban made Jacob work seven years for each wife,
Deceived Jacob by giving Leah, not Rachel, as his first bride.[58]

---

57. Ibid., 25:29–34.
58. Ibid., 29:15–30.

But Jacob cheated his uncle in multiplying his own flocks;[59]
Arranged to run away,[60] and Rachel stole the family's 'gods.'[61]
Laban eventually caught him, but sent him on his way.
Laban saw himself in young Jacob, therefore let him go free.[62]

Each recognized in the other a masterful Deceiver;
They parted as equals, but not wanting to see each other.
Now Jacob is going home: back to where deceit started.
He's contemplating his behavior, can't disregard it.
He projects his own inner judge onto his brother Esau,
Thus is terrified to meet him, then encounters the angel.

In wrestling with the angel, Jacob looks within.
He'd been living out his shadow, thought it was him!
Probably thought that the angel was God punishing him,
To show him who's boss, certainly not coming to befriend.
But this spirit didn't disempower, didn't humiliate;
Rather so affirmed Jacob's strength, it gave him a new name.

The name 'Jacob' meant 'Supplanter'; he'd grabbed Esau's heel,[63]
As if already in childbirth, the birthright he'd steal.
That's what his parents focused on, as he entered this world:
He was named 'The Supplanter,' and so his story unfurled.
Defined thus by his parents, he remained close to his mother,
Who used him for her own ends, as a pawn in her battle.

Who is a person anyway, what's one's identity?
It's how one is seen by one's parents, at least initially.
Part of Jacob's journey to become his own person
Is living out his mother's shadow, which is also his own.
Their conspiracy of deceit, though, means he'll have to flee;
But by then, even on his own, it's his identity.

---

59. Ibid., 30:25–43.
60. Ibid., 31:1–21.
61. Ibid., 31:19, 33–35.
62. Ibid., 31:22–55.
63. Ibid., 25:19–28.

The angel asks him his name, and he says who he is.
'You'll no longer be identified as that, but as this,'
Says the angel; 'Your new name is "Israel"; I'll tell you why:
You've striven with God and humans, and you've survived!'
Then naturally enough, Jacob asks 'What is your name?'
But the angel asked 'Why ask?' And there he blessed him.[64]

What a tender sweet moment: such intimacy;
Jacob wanted to be even closer, he couldn't quite yet see
That the Presence he was dealing with was already in him,
While greater than him also, and not limited by a name.
Jacob wouldn't be controlling it by the handle of a name;
The Spirit was now inside Jacob, making him a new man.

So the angel disappeared, setting both of them free,
Because Jacob no longer fought it; inside he let it be.
Inversely, Jacob's shadow had actually been the light,
Which he hadn't come to know until the wrestling at midnight.
He'd discovered in that encounter a much greater power
Than his ego could wield; plus he'd be alone no more.

In awe at what had happened, sensing his old self had died,
He focused not on that death, but on still being alive!
The words that he uttered usually move me to tears:
'I have seen God face to face, and yet my life is preserved.'
He called that place 'Peniel,' which means 'The face of God.'[65]
He walked away with a limp, but full of the Spirit inside.

Next day he sees Esau, and with him four-hundred men;
Jacob's old fears die hard: he fears that this is the end.[66]
Within his old paradigm, he figures he has to pay,
That Esau is vindictive, bearing a grudge to this day.
He of course doesn't know yet how else it could play out,
But he's already a changed man, with a different approach.

---

64. Ibid., 32:27–29.
65. Ibid., 32:30 (notice Bible footnote "*l*").
66. Ibid., 33:1–3.

He uses less of his energy trying to be in control,
Both physically and spiritually, he trusts being vulnerable.
He bows down seven times, as his brother rides up,[67]
Afraid to the last minute of what will happen next.
Esau jumps down from his camel, and rushes to greet him;
Throws his arms around Jacob, and they embrace, weeping.[68]

As so often in scripture, and in spiritual stories,
Transformation is made real in human encounters.
Even internal change, such as Jacob's at Peniel,
Or mine at midnight, in wrestling with the devil,
Aren't fully made real until they're validated,
Which happens uncannily –a reflection of inner change.

Thus when Esau greets Jacob, and embodies forgiveness,
Jacob's profoundly moved, saying, 'Truly seeing your face
Is like seeing God's face, you've shown me such favor.'[69]
As with God, so with Esau, he'd thought he would die,
But instead he found love, and a blessed new life.
Both inside and out, his new being was validated.

Esau, with a full heart, wants to travel together,[70]
To join the two companies, the reunion to savor.
Jacob too is grateful, but sensitively protests:
"My wives, children, and flocks are slow and need rest."[71]
Esau initially declines all the gifts Jacob offers;[72]
The best gift—brother love—they've already given each other.

What's happening here," Grandpa says, "is once again moving:
Each will go his separate way, but with each other's blessing.
I didn't have an Esau, not exactly, you see,
To validate—after my wrestling—the new man in me.

    67. Ibid., 33:3.
    68. Ibid., 33:4.
    69. Ibid., 33:10.
    70. Ibid., 33:12.
    71. Ibid., 33:13–15.
    72. Ibid., 33:9–11.

But I gradually came to realize, on subsequent nights,
That God had blessed me too, and I'd be all right.

My relationship with God has since been on new footing;
Like Jacob, I too, have been on a spiritual journey.
No longer locked in combat over who's in control,
I've let go of my demands and though armless, I'm whole!
I feel loved, am more humble, am aware of my place,
I'm less willful, more trusting, alive with God's grace.

Yes, the loss of my arm was a painful price to pay;
But I'm not sure I'd have changed by any other way.
Like Jacob with his limp, my loss reminds me daily
That when I trust God, like Jesus, the devil gets behind me.[73]
Strength is not just being strong, but being Spirit-full,
Which means my ego will die, but not I when I'm vulnerable.

I've already learned new ways of being alive;
I miss my arm terribly, but I'm being creative.
I can no longer do some things other men can,
But neither competition nor control define a man.
I'm grateful beyond words to be telling this story;
I can work, pray, and sing, and give God the glory!"

---

73. Op. cit., Matthew 16:23.

Uncle Charlie's Funeral

His casket's rolled in front of the altar
In the church that was his spiritual home.
I'm attending Uncle Charlie's funeral:
Perfect place from which he'll be launched.

I've known him for over twenty years,
Been welcomed into his heart and home.
Talking about church would move him to tears,
Like very few men that I've known.

Mechanical engineering was his trade;
He was also a U. S. Army Veteran.
He was grateful but also ashamed,
That he'd never seen literal war action.

Grateful owner of his modest Flushing home,
He was hospitable in an easy-going way.
He knew what he should and shouldn't eat,
But he was usually a little paunchy anyway.

When my wife and I talked of where we'd been
In the greater metropolitan region,
He'd say "There's a bridge there I helped design."
He was proud of his life's contribution.

One bridge he specifically mentioned
Was over Carnegie Lake going into Princeton,
Where I did my theological education;
So whenever I'd cross it I'd think of him.

He was married to my wife's Aunt Arlene:
Was therefore my uncle by marriage;
In many ways I felt like his son,
Definitely a spiritual companion.

I'd come to know he was an only child,
But he never mentioned his parents.
World War Two had been over quite a while,
But maybe they felt uneasy being Germans.

His oldest son had graduated from college,
Moved to Pittsburgh, and taught high school music.
He kept his distance, which he then consolidated
By marrying a devout hypocritical shrew.

She blinded herself to her own shadow side
By focusing on the flaws of his parents.
So by choosing a woman like this as his bride,
Charles Junior had married his own shadow anger.

Charlie barely got to know his grandchildren,
And I wondered what this rift was about;
Then I heard from my wife and Aunt Arlene
Charlie had slapped young Charles around.

This relationship with his eldest son
Brings to mind that biblical declaration
About God visiting the iniquity of the fathers
Upon the third and the fourth generations."[74]

Young Charles did inherit the iniquity,
Which got in the way of feeling his dad's love;
But Charlie sought and received forgiveness anyway,
And from God's love Uncle Charlie wouldn't be moved.

His younger son did not attend college;
But lived at home until nearly age thirty.
He built a room for himself in their basement,
Worked for the traffic department of New York City.

He moved out and got married in his thirties,
Then died of a heart attack at age thirty-nine!
Aunt Arlene and Uncle Charlie were devastated.
Charlie doubted that he'd ever again be fine.

  74. The Holy Bible (RSV), Exodus 20:5b–6.

Though at first he felt desolate and betrayed,
It was from the church he received the most comfort.
He was definitely angry with God,
But that relationship was not ultimately undone.

Kenny's death, though, and my uncle's being fired
From his job a few years before retirement,
Left him questioning the values he'd held,
And stripped of any spiritual entitlement.

He'd believed one should be rewarded for hard work,
And that life is—or somehow should be—fair;
But Faith told him that God's thoughts aren't like ours,[75]
Which kept him from ultimate despair.

Not long after Kenny's death he had a stroke,
Leaving him quite paralyzed on his right side.
He worked hard to get his functioning back,
But I think he felt broken deep inside.

He never fully recovered from the stroke,
After the lay-off and the death of his son.
These were seriously unsettling blows
Which left him declined towards depression.

But he enjoyed sitting out on his porch,
Chatting with neighbors from India next door:
And when he reflected on his life as a whole,
He was grateful for God's love at the core.

A couple years later, he died.
His eldest son even then kept his distance;
To attend his father's funeral he felt obliged,
But he had to overcome inner resistance.

I sorted through my uncle's tools in his basement,
But I eerily felt at times that I was grave-robbing:
That the tools I was touching were his bones,
Still animated by his spirit, though disembodied.

75. Op. cit., Isaiah 55:8–9.

I was so glad that the funeral was in a church,
Where death is dealt with in the larger context
Of our being enlivened by the breath of God,
Commending to God's hands our spirit at death.[76]

In church, then, can mourners deeply grieve,
Trusting that in God they'll find ultimate comfort.
In this church I felt welcomed and received,
Upheld in sorrow by their spiritual fellowship.

I wept as the Funeral Service unfolded.
The Pastor paid tribute to Charlie's life and faith,
Thanking God for God's forgiving love and
Charlie for bearing witness to God's grace;

For his faithfulness, humility, hospitality,
For his generosity and eagerness to help,
For his being a dependable part of that community,
Even too often putting others ahead of himself.

The context of sanctuary, worship, and eulogy
Upheld me, let me be lost in my grief.
Thus absorbed, I heard angels singing!
"Kyrie eleison, Christe eleison, Kyrie eleison."

Was this happening inside my head, outside, or both?
"Lord have mercy, Christ have mercy, Lord have mercy."
I turned and saw it was the church's small choir
Walking up and down the aisles singing sweetly,

Asking God to receive with mercy the soul
Of this dearly departed sinner and saint.
I was so moved I almost burst aloud with joy!
In a trance, I saw the coffin become a ship:

A ship borne aloft on the air,
Bearing Uncle Charlie away to his home.
I wanted the choir to keep singing forever,
I never wanted this experience to end.

    76. Op. cit., Luke 23:46.

Those words bridged the space and time gap
Between us body-bound creatures and beyond.
The singing stopped but not in my heart.
I came down from my mount of transfiguration.[77]

Roused from wanting to dwell there forever,
As the Service drew to a close I had to get up.
Feeling like a zombie, I had to recover,
And leave the sanctuary without any help.

My image of that airborne ship coffin
Reminded me of Elisha seeing Elijah
Caught up from earth while they were walking
By a chariot and horses of fire.[78]

Holy Spirit caught up Charlie's spirit that day.
Like Elisha, I too was a witness.
Elisha cried out "My father, my father!
The chariots of Israel and its horsemen!"[79]

I wish I too had burst out with something!
Even if on its face it hadn't made much sense:
How can one expect to be comprehensible?
My God, I was experiencing Transcendence!

As I stumbled and re-entered the mundane,
My heart was sad but even deeper still singing.
What was outside was now clearly within:
Through Charlie I received an ongoing blessing.

---

77. Op. cit., Mark 9:2–8.
78. Op. cit., II Kings 2:9–14.
79. Ibid., 2:12.

Kingdom of Heaven: Still At Hand?

What in the world does it mean today
That "the kingdom of heaven is at hand?"[80]
There are no kings nor kingdoms per se,
So what could it mean from where we stand?

Yet the negative linguistic analogy—
No earthly kingdom but a heavenly one—
Resonates deeply and invites us to see
The presence of an invisible reality.

But before it begins to make some sense,
We hear the prefacing "Repent!"
Which rings of judgment, remonstrance,
Which human pride is sure to resent.

Human pride resents "Repent!"
Which means "Be penitent again."
But was I ever penitent?
To live my way is my intent.

But Baptist John does not relent;
In the wilderness he cries "Repent!"
When hearers ask him who he is
Inquire of him by whom he's sent,

He answers not about descent,
But in rugged garments all but rent
He speaks in ancient prophets' lore
That he's the one who's sent before

---

80. The Holy Bible (RSV), Matthew 3:2

The Anointed One who's soon to follow.
John quotes the ancient sacred text,
Which places the present in the context
Of sacred action prior, now, and next.

Concerning who he is, his identity,
He says, Look for the one who comes after me.
His shoes to untie I am not worthy,
Pointing to him is what defines me.[81]

John's very existence is a metaphor:
He is who he is and a whole lot more.
He dresses and lives in a different place,
Playing with our notions of time and space.

The voice, the voice is who I am,
Crying in the wilderness, "Make way for him
By making straight your crooked ways":
Think of God, not your selfish craze.

John's whole way of living was part of his "voice";
His outlandish ways got people's attention.
He dressed and ate weirdly by deliberate choice,
Living in the wilderness to be outside convention.

Another thing he did that was catchy wild:
He turned topsy turvy confession and denial.
By confessing not denying that he's NOT the Messiah,
He asserts his role to be pointing to Messiah.[82]

He tweaked people's hopes for the Anointed One,
Drawing on their longing for God's own Son
Who would come and deliver them from all their foes,
And heal and protect them from all their woes.

---

81. Op. cit., Matthew 3:1–11; Mark 1:1–8; Luke 3:1–20; John 1:19–27.
82. Op. cit., John 1:19–20.

Their thoughts were fixed on the world outside,
On an earthly kingdom which would give them pride.
John knew and cut through how they thought about God:
That God's part of them, not them part of God.

Like most human beings, we stake a special claim
That God will serve us no matter how vain;
That we need do nothing to be spiritually mature,
That birth and family lineage our specialness ensure.[83]

But John will have none of this: it makes him angry;
He's a voice for God's wrath and divine desire,
Proclaiming that the ax is at the root of the tree:
If it doesn't bear good fruit it'll be thrown in the fire.[84]

The crowds ask John, "Then what shall we do?"
His answer brings us back to our opening question:
The answer isn't hard if we're honest and true,
If we're humble and open to divine reflection.

Share with the poor your clothes and your food.
Even Wall Streeters ask, "Teacher, what shall we do?"
Collect no more than the amount you're prescribed.
Soldiers: don't abuse power, extort, or bribe.[85]

Deep in their hearts people knew John was right;
They couldn't help but wonder if he was Messiah.
He consistently confessed that it was not him;
Baptism for repentance meant a change within.[86]

Look not outside for this kingdom at hand:
Be baptized, almost drown, then take a new breath.
Live your life differently, alive from within,
Reconnected with God, choosing life not death.

---

83. Op. cit. Matthew 3:1–9; Luke 3:7–8.
84. Op. cit., Matthew 3:10; Luke 3:9.
85. Op. cit., Luke 3:10–14
86. Op. cit., Luke 3:15–17.

The kingdom is at hand in every breath and action.
Your ego's fear of death actually blocks new life.
By denying a higher power you delude yourself,
Not surrendering to God, with anxiety you're rife.

To repent and be baptized are one's individual choice;
But one must take action and not just coast.
To one's pride, greed, and selfishness one must give voice,
Such honesty helps us not be grandiose.

In modern terms we'd say, "Don't deny your shadow."
Be honest with yourself: your wish to dominate;
How resistant you are to change your direction;
How selfish you are in the ways you relate.

God's overall goal isn't judgment: it's love.
To embrace God within is to be more alive.
But God's life within involves ego sacrifice:
The death of what is, allows for more abundant life.

II

The forms this process takes are myriad to see:
How inner and outer forces resist such change.
Parents cripple their children to seek security.
Fear fights trusting God our life to arrange.

A mother finds peace with a baby at her breast,
But she nurses way too long—her own needs to feed;
To fill her empty life she curbs baby's separateness,
So the baby learns quite early to feed his mother's needs.

His tiniest little moves towards self-autonomy
Evoke fears of loneliness she thinks she can't bear.
She heightens fears of life disproportionately,
Thus undermining his confidence to function out there.

She blunts her own life by defining self as mother,
Using the power of that role to feel in control.
But it's all an elaborate, self-deluding cover
For denying her need of God to feel truly whole.

We're all strongly tempted to deny our condition
As creatures who are nothing unconnected to God.
So intent to be kings of an earthly kingdom,
We deny our vulnerability, we try to be God.

The father of the child just wants to have sex;
He's feeling left out and has his needs too!
When his wife says no, that she's not ready yet,
He feels rejected and angry, unsure what to do.

He's faintly aware of what gets triggered by the baby:
An infant inside him wants to be held and suckle;
But he doesn't want to accept that he's feeling envy;
And to avoid feeling helpless he can withdraw and sulk.

His own infant feelings, which as an infant he repressed,
Get reactivated by baby's primitive cries.
He's coped by shutting down the cries he couldn't express;
Now the baby giving voice to them takes him by surprise.

He wants to hit the baby, to stop its desperate cries.
Rather than feel vulnerable, he decides to dominate.
Can't comfort self or baby no matter what he tries;
Never learned to bear his own pain: can't help the little mate.

He's frustrated and angry, won't acknowledge his needs;
Takes it all personally and thinks he's entitled.
He yells at the baby, or his wife, or he pleads—
Which leaves him more lonely and frightened deep inside.

Neither mother nor father can step outside their ego;
Their feelings are normal and indeed hard to bear;
They haven't learned that loving is bigger than one's ego,
That maturing in the Spirit means suffering to bear.

III

In this respect, too, the biblical infant stories—
Which we're too quick to think are exceptions to the rule—
Place births in the context of a much bigger story
In which each person is precious but egos don't rule.

Just remember the story of Jesus, Joseph, Mary:
Joseph's not the father and could feel like a duped fool.[87]
Mary could be frightened by her unexpected pregnancy,[88]
But accepts being God's handmaiden and sings about it too![89]

When twelve-year-old Jesus stays behind in the Temple,
He hears from his parents what their egos went through.
"Why have you treated us like this?" they say for example;
"You've caused us great anxiety, we were looking for you!"

The way Jesus answers must have filled them with wonder:
Why were you searching? How could you not know?
Don't you remember that it's God's who's my ultimate father?
He's the one I'm loyal to, "it's about his business I go."

They didn't understand him, and it must have hurt;
Their parenting had limits; he wasn't their, their child.
But Jesus did respect them: he returned home obedient.
Mary pondered in her heart everything that he'd said.[90]

Prior to John the Baptist's birth, his mother had been barren;
Then appeared an angel to her husband Zechariah,
Saying, Your prayers have been heard, you will soon have a son.
He will be great before the Lord, with the power of Elijah.

---

87. Op. cit., Matthew 1:18–25; Luke 2:1–20.
88. Op. cit. Luke 1:26–38.
89. Op. cit., Luke 1:46–55.
90. Op. cit., Luke 2:41–51.

Because he and Elizabeth were getting on in years,
He said to the angel, "How will I know that this is so?"
The angel said, It's God who sent me with this news;
Your doubts will leave you mute till the baby appears.[91]

Already the Holy Spirit was at work with John's father,
A priest in the world of institutional religion:
The Spirit will intervene, even seem like a bother,
Exploding ritual habits as the new thing comes in.

IV

One point of these stories is to help us to see
That not only in the past but also here and now:
Being open to God's presence is how we can choose to be,
Opening our hearts to what it is that God wants us to know.

These stories also teach us that God's presence is scary,
That our egos are threatened when they're not in control.
That for change, death, and suffering we must all be ready,
As Simeon said to Mary, "A sword will pierce your own soul."

May we all know a Simeon, a devout holy man,
Who guided by the Spirit, helps us to see divine birth;
Amazing us yet reminding us that we oppose God within
So that our inner thoughts about God may all be laid bare.[92]

Once we see our own resistance, once that's out and laid bare,
We're then outside our ego, able to see ourselves whole.
We'll know that choosing Spirit will mean loss to the ego,
But that living our life as God wants it, our joy will be full.

An ego that's humble, open to change and pain,
Can see this kingdom, this alternate domain.
This ego will die, can even see it as gain:
Holy Spirit and fire will refine and sustain.

    91. Op. cit., Luke 1:5–24.
    92. The Holy Bible (NRSV)., Luke 2:25–35.

V

John's spiritual integrity is a thing of great awe:
Establishment religion tries to take him down;
They attack him for ignoring ritual law,
Thinking obedience to that is what makes a man sound.[93]

John's very own disciples then appeal to his envy,
That the very thing he prophesied is now coming true!
"That he who comes after me ranks before me,"
"All are going to [Jesus]," now what shall we do?[94]

John's answer keeps us focused on the heart of this story:
John lives what he says his entire life through.
Life's not about ego, it's about divine glory,
My relationship with God determines what I do.

John calmly reminds them what they heard from the start:
I am not the Messiah but I was sent ahead.[95]
What you're seeing now is an unfolding part:
"That he must increase, I must decrease instead."

It's poignant to hear John as he's spelling this out.
Won't he give himself just a little bit of credit?
What he adds next makes the listener want to shout:
He talks of joy and fulfillment when we least expect it!

He stays focused on God, keeps things in perspective.
That he's the Best Man, not the groom of the bride.[96]
As John stands by, sees what's happening with Jesus:
Hearing the voice of Jesus he can set his own voice aside.

---

93. Op. cit., John 3:25.
94. Op. cit., John 3:26.
95. Op. cit., John 3:30.
96. Op. cit., John 3:29.

With great joy he does this, seeing his ministry fulfilled.[97]
But he has some last words of generosity and love;
He expands our understanding in a way that we're thrilled:
It's not a "him or me" thing but God's word from above.

Thus he sings next some words among the best in the Bible;
He makes note of it twice that they come from above:
"He whom God has sent speaks the [very] words of God,
For he gives the Spirit without measure" and unrestrained love.[98]

We can imagine John's journey as he voices these words;
He can speak either earthly things or things from above.[99]
These words emerge with wisdom from his daily human struggle,
From his personal experience of unbounded grace and love.

John's discovered that God's word is a living event,
That what communicates God's word is a life in the flesh.
That one who lives out the word he has heard, seen, or felt
May suffer as a prophet but by God is blessed.

John is careful with words because he knows they're intense;
He knows in himself when his life is God's Word.
When he's a living human document giving voice to God's presence,[100]
His words are then a medium and his body God's abode.

People recognize God's presence in themselves or another,
And by accepting that presence they attest that God is true.
God's Spirit is not limited to one and not another;
Eternal life is available and everything's then new.

---

97. Op. cit., John 3:29.
98. Op. cit., John 3:34–35 (emphasis mine).
99. Op. cit., John 3:33.
100. Gerkin, Charles V., The Living Human Document, Abingdon Press, 1984.

John's life and his words reveal the kingdom of heaven;
He announces and lives out that the kingdom is at hand;
That God's Spirit is the Source of the life we are given,
That a penitent ego is what we need with God to stand.

VI

Now back to our story about Jesus and John,
The relationship between them is an example to behold!
John's disciples ask Jesus if he's the one who's to come?
Jesus said, Tell John all the healing that you've seen and heard.[101]

But Jesus spoke to the crowds then about the Baptist's power:
Whom did you go out to see, "a reed shaken by the wind?"
Or someone dressed in fancy clothes and in a royal palace?
No, a prophet; yes, "more than a prophet," whom God did send.[102]

"I tell you," said Jesus, There's none greater than he.
But lest you hear me saying that he's greater than you,
In the Kingdom of God there's a different economy:
There's no greater or least: it's God's will we all do.[103]

The writer goes on, tries to made sure that Readers get it:
Through repentance and baptism we enter the kingdom;
We either die to our ego, accept that on God we're dependent,
Or we're like those who thwart what God had in mind for them. [104]

VII

But amidst all this talk of God's life and God's love,
What then shall we make of the reality of death?
Doesn't it silence the kingdom and all talk of "above"
When bodies decay, words die with one's last breath?

---

101. Op. cit., Matthew 11:2-6.
102. Op. cit., Matthew 11:7-10; Luke 7:24-27.
103. Op. cit. Matthew 11:11; Luke 7:28.
104. The Jerusalem Bible, Luke 7:30.

John's metaphor-life of voicing God's presence
Continues through his death cause his death speaks too.
By pointing beyond himself he knew that his disappearance
Would be part of God's message that was still coming through.

John confronted King Herod with abusing his power
By taking for himself his own brother's wife.
Herod threw John in prison, then stooped even lower
By having John beheaded at the whim of this wife.[105]

John lived what he spoke in this final way, too.
He died confronting Power with ultimate Truth.
After having John killed, Herod feared he had risen,
And that the powers Jesus had, he had for this reason!

Irony's at the heart of this Kingdom of Heaven
Surrendering to death is a part of whole life.
John's death proclaiming God becomes holy leaven;
Though John himself die, God's message will live.

The most powerful tribute that John's life was true—
That John's life is a story told for us by God—
Is that Jesus' ministry begins with words that aren't new:
He says, "Repent, for the kingdom of heaven is at hand!!!"[106]

He takes up John's words and lives them more fully.
John pointed beyond himself by pointing to another;
Jesus' actions, words, and being point to God more wholly:
Beyond himself indeed, but also alive within forever.

His mother was God's handmaid, she knew it from the start.
His father also knew he wasn't his biological son.
This child wasn't theirs; he'd follow his own heart.
Their relationship with God helped them follow God's plan.

---

105. The Holy Bible (NRSV), Matthew 14:1–12.
106. The Holy Bible (RSV)., Matthew 4:17; Mark 1:14.

VIII

So what are we learning about the kingdom of heaven?
What relevance does it have for our lives today?
The heart of the matter is the kind of life we're living:
Do we communicate with our lives what God wants to say?

But you've heard that before, to the point that it's boring,
And anyone can say they've got a corner on God.
Goldman Sachs' Blankfein can say "It's God's work I'm doing":[107]
He's ego-drunk with what power comes from usury and greed.

By their fruits shall you know them, we hear Jesus say.[108]
Their lips say "Lord, Lord," but their hearts are far from me.[109]
They turn things upside down: regard the potter as the clay,
The vessel made says of the maker, "He did not make me."[110]

From heart's treasure the good person good deeds will display,[111]
How you relate to "the least" reveals your relationship with me.[112]
The "prosperity gospel" builds on how Jabez proudly prayed:[113]
False prophets try to deny the ego's basic insecurity.[114]

Jesus' disciples themselves were vulnerable to inflation;
At one point they were arguing over who was the greater.
Overhearing them Jesus explained that in God's kingdom
The leader is a servant and the older like the younger.[115]

---

107. Google Search for "Blankfein god's work."
108. The Holy Bible (NRSV), Matthew 7:16, 20.
109. Op. cit., Matthew 15:8–9; Matthew 7:21.
110. Op. cit., Isaiah 29:16.
111. Op. cit., Luke 6:45.
112. Op. cit., Matthew 25:40.
113. Op. cit., I Chronicles 4:10.
114. Op. cit., Matthew 7:15.
115. Op. cit., Luke 22:24–26.

Then again Jesus' disciples were stern and highhanded
When people brought infants that Jesus might touch them.
But Jesus was angry at his disciples and commanded,
"Let the little children come to me and do not stop them,

For it is to such as these that the kingdom of God belongs."
"Truly," he went on, as he them took them in his arms,
"Whoever does not receive the kingdom of God as a little child
Will never enter it." He blessed them and moved on.[116]

The themes here again are relationship, dependence.
As humans we're dependent upon our Creator for breath.
Like children we're also always growing towards independence,
But like Jesus we call God "Father" even upon our death.

Perhaps the most lyrical summary of all of this
Is oft called "The Song of Christ" in Philippians 2.
It's an inspiring example of how words capture bliss,
But the whole journey includes death and emptiness too.

At the heart of kingdom living is humility,
Which makes contact possible with the heart of another:
Do nothing from selfish ambition or conceit,
Do not regard yourself ever better than the other.

God's life in Jesus makes clear for the seeing:
Equality with God, Jesus didn't exploit.
He humbled himself and became a whole human being,
All the way to death, to God he was obedient.[117]

Like John he trusted too in life beyond ego;
But his words also reveal what his ego went through.
Feeling betrayed upon the cross, he cried God why forsake me?[118]
But with his last breath, Father, I commend my spirit to you.[119]

---

116. Op. cit., Matthew 18:13–15; Luke 18:15–17.
117. Op. cit., Philippians 2:1–11.
118. Op. cit., Mark 15:34.
119. Op. cit., Luke 23:46.

Look each "not to your own interests," continues St. Paul,
"But to the interest of others," in compassion, sympathy;[120]
Be assured that your egos will need lots of support,
Because life in the Spirit means ego insecurity.

The powers-that-be won't want to hear at all
That their power is fleeting and just temporary.
The lives of the saints give consistent reports
Of egos fighting surrender or escaping into sleep.[121]

IX

Created by God we need God's Spirit for life.
Egos get formed through identification and opposition;
Through this rhythm one arrives at an autonomous self,
And in the end one goes one's own way or lives life as one chosen.

When ego goes its own way, it thinks it's in control.
In some ways it is; it was created with free will.
But then self-preservation becomes its primary goal,
Along with denying inner emptiness it can never fully fill.

Instead of humbly acknowledging its dependence on Spirit,
It seeks power over others and doubtless certainty;
Self-righteous it can be, cruel, and even violent,
Choosing manipulation and domination over vulnerability.

Jesus' words in this regard at first make no sense:
That since John began proclaiming "the kingdom is at hand,"
The kingdom of heaven has been suffering violence;[122]
Rather than repent, people try to force God's hand.

---

120. Op. cit., Philippians 2:1–4
121. Op. cit., Matthew 26:40–46; Mark 14:37–42; Luke 22:45–46.
122. Op. cit., Matthew 11:12; Luke 16:16–17.

When ego feels threatened, it tries to take over,
To dominate rather than its limits to concede;
Or when it sees in others what in self it tries to cover,
It's capable of astounding acts of cold brutality.

When confronted with its pride, the ego has a choice:
To alter its ways and get aligned right with God,
Or do as Cain who envied God's pleasure with Abel's sacrifice,
Struck out and killed Abel instead of getting right with God.[123]

We all do indeed try to take God by force;
When things don't go our own way, we can lash out and hurt;
There's a Cain,[124] David,[125] Paul[126] in the heart of each one of us:
We feel murderous rage and we're sure we're in the right.

In this respect, too, think of Emperor Constantine,
Who was converted, okay; but to conquer the world?
And current so-called Christians who want theocracy,
Like Crusaders would kill all Muslims if only they could.

"The violent take it by force":[127] oh, yes, it's still done.
Glaring self-interest, "shock and awe," "liberation";
Imposing "democracy" with bombs dropped by a drone.
A far cry from "not by might, nor by power, but my Spirit" alone.[128]

We've become so inured that it hardly even shocks us
When one human being takes the life of another!
What could account for such astonishing arrogance
Than that the ego exalts itself above God and all others.

---

123. Op. cit., Genesis 4:1–8.
124. Loc. cit.
125. Op. cit., II Samuel 11:1–21.
126. Op. cit., Acts 7:58; Acts 8:1–3.
127. Op. cit., Matthew 11:12b.
128. Op. cit., Zechariah 4:6.

Proud egos can resist God through blatant defiance:
This form of rebellion is easiest to see.
A more subtle form is craven cowardice
Which denies all resistance and bows abjectly.

The former denies fear; the latter is ruled by it.
The latter tries to avoid taking responsibility
For discovering one's own strength, even through doubt,
Then committing wholeheartedly to either self or Spirit.

The arrogance of the former is frightening to see:
To murder, war, and mayhem they give hardly a thought.
They may be successful, even admired for all they've got,
But their hardness of heart leads to global tragedy.

But the docile are dangerous in their craven passivity.
They probably believe in classic atonement theory:
That Jesus' suffering and death were all done for me
So that from all that, God will mercifully spare me.

But where is God's mercy then in killing God's own son?
That's a divinely-sanctioned version of human sacrifice!
Perhaps what Jesus did *for* us was meant to be education:
That God's love shows that ego death can lead to new life.

Jesus made clear that he's the Way, the Truth, the Life;[129]
That we must do our own suffering in following him.
He and John show clearly how to live in the kingdom,
We must die to our own selves, not be bailed out by them.[130]

Now, Jesus, like us, didn't look forward to death;
He prayed fervently to God "Remove this cup from me."[131]
But much stronger than his fear was being fully alive,
Showing how God's life breaks all bonds, continually.

---

129. Op. cit., John 14:6a.
130. Op. cit., Matthew 16:24-25.
131. Op. cit., Matthew 26:36-39; Mark 14:32-36; Luke 22:39-44.

X

One wonders if human selfishness ever will end.
Will it make any difference that the kingdom is at hand?
We return to where we started: only if people "Repent!"
Because life in God's Kingdom is the world's only hope.

It's hard to put ego in spiritual perspective;
Doing so only highlights yet another irony:
It takes a strong—not weak—ego to handle Holy Spirit,
To do justice, love mercy, and walk with God humbly.

We're called in Jesus' absence to "work out our own salvation"—
Our wholeness, that is, in relationship with God—
Our egos will do it with fear and with trembling,
"For God is at work in [us] both to will and to work."[132]

Life conscious of God doesn't sound like much fun;
Why would anyone choose it, and what's the reward?
One doesn't really choose it; by the Spirit one's chosen,
But then the fullness one feels is joy beyond words.

Openness to Spirit—realizing: *That's What we're breathing!*—
Gives us courage to face anything, grateful for each breath,
Knowing that God's love is the reason everything's existing;
From that love nothing separates us in life or in death.[133]

---

132. Op. cit., Philippians 2:12-13.
133. Op. cit., Romans 8:38-39.

God Stammers with Longing, Then Shows Sacrificial Love

One day,
Her right breast
Pressed against my left,
The sides of our faces touching
During a routine
Goodbye hug,
My right hand
Lightly grazed
Her left breast
As I withdrew
My hand from
Around her shoulder
As we stepped apart.

I'm still there.

The voltage
Of that touch
Emblazoned
A neural pathway
In my being
That still surges.
My heart pounds,
My body swells,
Whenever I think
Of that brush with her.

Why such a charge?

Sexual sparks, definitely!
Lust for forbidden fruit? Yes!

A desire for more? O my, yes!
Greater intimacy? Yes again!
Wanting more
At all these levels.

The intensity
Partly to be accounted for
By the condensation
Of miles and miles of
Conversation on the
Years-long road of
Our relationship.
All that's packed and
Held between us
Hissed and crackled
With sparks
Like the exposed ends
Of two hot live wires
Momentarily touching.

Wanting more, yes,
At all those levels.
But also aware
That this was
A brush with mystery:
A hot-wire connection
Between and beyond
Our boundaried,
Insulated selves.
Each of us knows
There's so much
Still unknown,
Which will always be
Unknown yet sensed.
Much would remain
Holy and beyond ken
Even were we to try

To get to know
Each other better still.

We're embodied sexual beings
Enlivened by that Spirit
Which brooded over fecund waters
Until that procreative Spirit
Breathed into us
The sacred breath of life.

Spirit animates body,
Invisible moves visible,
Mystery, glimpsed
While hidden,
Ignites fascination and
Opens one to transcendence.

The Lord used to speak
To Moses face to face,
As one speaks to a friend.[134]

What a statement!

Yet Moses says,
  "Show me your glory, I pray."[135]
He wants more.

Hear then the exquisite tenderness
Of the Lord stammering in reply:[136]
"I will make all my goodness
Pass before you,
And will proclaim before you
The name 'The Lord';
And I will be gracious
To whom I will be gracious,

---

134. The Holy Bible (NRSV), Exodus 33:11a.

135. Ibid., 33:18.

136. Cf. Op.cit., 4:10–17: Moses said that he is "slow of speech and tongue" [stutters?] when he resisted God's call.

And will show mercy
On whom I will show mercy.
But," the Lord said,
"You cannot see my face;
For no one shall see me and live."[137]

That seems to be the end of it.
If we get too close, we'll die:
Our separateness will disappear.

But wait. Listen!
That's not the final word.
God too wants more!!
The successive staccato
Declarations of identity
And autonomy
Reveal a divine struggle
Between a longing
For fuller intimacy
Yet at the same time
Wanting to neither lose oneself
Nor devour the other.

"I will do this . . . and I will give that;
I will be this . . . and I will show that,
But you cannot see my face."

But, . . . there's more:
"The Lord continued,
'See, there is a place by me
Where you shall stand on the rock;

And while my glory passes by
I will put you in a cleft of the rock,
And I will cover you with my hand, . . .
And you shall see my back;
But my face shall not be seen.'"[138]

137. Ibid., 33:19–20.
138. Ibid., 33:21–22.

It's hard to find
A more vulnerable
Offer of greater intimacy
While preserving individuality
In the entire Bible.

God gives all God can, and more,
While at the same time,
God sacrifices God's own desire
For even greater intimacy
Because of God's love
For the separate existence
Of the beloved other.

So we meet, too, face to face,
Or hand brushing breast,
As one relates with a friend:
We see the other's face,
But at the same time,
Because of both the
Brilliant blinding intensity,
And the devouring deadly darkness
Of all that lies behind a face,
We protect ourselves and others
From the fullness of our fiery being,
And our faces cannot be seen.
We can't see everything that's there
In or behind a face.
Faces are seen but not seen.

But we can live with longing and gratitude:
Wanting more,
Respectful of the other,
Grateful for all we have,
Praying to relate unselfishly
With divine sacrificial love.

Something That's Just Mine?
or God's Not Even Like That

"Damn it!
Can't I have something
That's just mine?"

I felt stricken
By the pain in his voice
More than the curse.

Some fifty years later
I can still conjure up
The shock in my gut:

The nascent recognition
That my provider Dad
Had needs of his own;

That those delicious
Bite-size Milky Way bars
In the refrigerator drawer

Weren't automatically
For me; that he, he
Wasn't only for me.

Shock, yes, and loss:
They felt taken away,
He seemed further away.

His verbal outburst
Over candy bars
Opened the abyss

Of existential isolation:
I was suddenly alone:
Had lost my innocence,

Had a hole in my gut,
A new-found guilt.
I felt indicted.

My inward protest
Of innocence, unvoiced,
Was undone by his pain.

But he didn't hit me
This time. He used words.
He held back his arm.

He endured some pain,
Expressed some in words,
Held what remained.

This too was a change:
Less physical contact,
Words bridged the gap.

The gap, yes, the gap.
I had to give back
Not candy bars, but work,

To pay my own way,
Carry my own weight:
This was the new state.

My worth was my own now,
No longer tied to his.
What now means love?

No longer enmeshed,
With my value assured,
Which I hadn't had to earn.

More on my own now,
I knew good and evil:
I'd eaten the apple.

In the sweat of his brow
Did Adam eat bread;
Outside of Eden now.

No mention of love
In that old Bible story.
But there is the fecund world.

The earth would bring forth,
Though containing a curse.
Things could have been worse.[139]

I still feared my Dad,
Now an internal judge:
Also how I knew God.

Off to college I left home:
Seventeen years old,
But I took home along.

In the years that ensued
I tried to earn love;
My impulses I feared.

I'd had hints of a love
Not based on what I did—
That I didn't have to earn:

Grandmother maternal,
Grandfather paternal,
Showed another love of me.

They delighted in me;
Of fear I felt free
In their company.

139. The Holy Bible (NRSV), Genesis 3.

Love deeper than what I did:
It wasn't even said:
I just knew they loved me:

Love prior to being good,
Love generously given.
Could this love be God?

But where lay my worth
If I didn't have to earn it?
Where'd this leave me?

If I could even be bad,
Still be loved by God,
What would guide me?

I'd be lost and alone
Though free and on my own:
What would guide me?

Should's and should-not's,
Of them I had a lot,
Oppressing me.

My ego felt besieged,
Could hardly breathe,
No spontaneity.

I lived in my head,
Did what I should:
God knows I was good;

Definitely depressed.
Even at my best,
Felt rather wooden.

II

In spite of this burden
Great Spirit was working
Deep inside of me.

I felt called to ministry;
Went to seminary:
Still lacked integrity.

I longed for more depth,
For some life-purpose,
Spiritual harmony.

I was all in my head,
Not grounded in my gut;
No whole identity.

I'd married for structure:
Outside of me,
And to have sex guilt-free.

Yes, there was some love,
But the marriage would prove
Unsatisfactory.

I sought wholeness there,
Thought connection to another
Would make me complete.

That "two become one"
I gradually came to see
Was quite unhealthy.

This codependency
Left neither of us free
To develop separate selves.

I wanted from her
What no human can give:
A spiritual love.

"Thank God for self-love"
Mose Allison says.
By his words I felt blessed![140]

Not narcissistic love
Where it's all about me;
But love of God in me.

It took years to mature,
And humility for sure,
To trust the Spirit in me.

I was still wracked by doubt,
I hadn't yet figured out
That it was okay to be me.

As a child I'd learned to hide;
Afraid of my Dad,
Danger always at hand:

Feared beatings by my Dad:
Much of the energy I had
I kept hidden and shut down,

Which left me depressed,
Afraid of an outburst,
Equally afraid of sex.

What's shut down so tightly
Becomes inwardly mighty,
Threatens to break free.

---

140. Allison, Mose, "Benediction," Tell Me Something: The Songs of Mose Allison, with Van Morrison, Exile Productions, Ltd., 1996.

III

At the age of twenty-three,
After Seminary,
I did a Summer of CPE.[141]

One decisive event,
A major turning point
In my spiritual journey:

I yelled at another—
A fellow peer-group member—
For acting high and mighty.

The Chaplain Supervisor
Validated my anger
By calling me "Tiger."

His delight in angry me
Began to set me free,
Unblock my energy.

I gradually began to see
That true love is free:
Loves me being me.

I could never earn love.
It's a gift one receives,
Then passes along freely.

This Chaplain judged me too,
But taught me what to do,
Which helped me to grow.

---

141. Clinical Pastoral Education: a program of supervised ministry in a setting such as Hospital Chaplaincy, prisons, etc.

IV

Transformation is slow,
But I was now on the road
To self-determinacy.

Pastoral Psychotherapy
Helped me understand me
In a context of safety.

Therapists cared about me
Which helped me to see me,
And face the shadow inside.

Unless I took a hard look—
Owned those dark parts of me—
They functioned independently.

When I owned them as mine,
Learned where they came from,
I was more at peace and calm.

I gradually felt lighter,
Much heaviness lifted,
My future seemed brighter.

As I faced how my anger
Would harshly judge Another
I came to know my father:

That I'd internalized my Dad
Related to others as he did,
Treated myself oppressively.

Just seeing this clearly,
My separate self got stronger,
Differentiated from father.

As my ego got stronger,
I began to reason with father,
Could modulate my anger.

I became less afraid
Of the sexual desires I had:
Could enjoy them instead.

Sex wasn't just intercourse,
Which remained important of course,
But was too narrow a focus.

Sex understood more broadly
As variable-voltage energy
Is embodied Spirituality.

Understood in this way,
One appreciates its power,
And how hard it is to handle.

How one deals with its power
Can become a metaphor
For how one relates to Life-Source:

I can think it's all mine
Grant my ego ultimacy,
Use sex as I please,

Focus only on my needs,
Meet them coercively,
Use others dispensably;

Which can only last so long
Since real life doesn't conform
To just meeting my needs.

Or else I can despair
Essentially give up
If I don't get what I want;

If I've had little control
Over how childhood unfolds
I have no hope left to lose.

Which leaves me a baby,
Passive, reactive,
Essentially whiny.

V

Either of these approaches
Can leave me feeling hopeless,
Either depressed or grandiose.

But if I encounter certain people
Who caringly support my ego,
While noting my limits also,

I can come to understand
That there's peace to be had
In humbly handling what's mine.

Can I have something just mine?
The answer's yes and no.
I'm one part of a whole.

What is mine is the choice
Of how I live my life:
With or without sacrifice.

Setting myself up as God
May seem a viable option,
But it's actually a mirage.

I don't own Life-Source
Nor can I take it by force.
Coercion doesn't last.

Nor is that who God is.
God is not dominant,
Nor relates as a tyrant.

I'm only fooling myself
And can do a lot of damage
Thinking of God in my image.

Where's that notion come from
That God reigns from top-down?
Demanding our obedience?

We're given a choice
Between seeing life as gift
Sustained by God's grace,

Or not considering God,
Not even thinking it's pride
Doing what's right in our own eyes.[142]

We're free to be arrogant,
To think this is all there is:
That there is no transcendence.

VI

What makes the difference for me
Is how well I breathe,
My degree of anxiety.

Differentiate one must
To find one's own self;
For a time one feels adrift.

Dad verbalized a boundary
Between himself and me
In that painful cry.

---

142. The Holy Bible (NRSV), Deuteronomy 12:8.

It started me on a journey
Towards seeking my security
Beyond any human being.

Launched by a parent.
Disappointed in a spouse,
At times desperate and lost,

Everything I'd been taught
Began to make sense to me,
Not just intellectually.

In therapy and CPE
I came to know God in me,
Recognize divine energy.

It's not something I possess,
And at times I neglect
To live in harmony;

Many times I ignore it,
Don't like its demands
If I choose for it.

It's a fearful thing indeed
To know the living God,
To fall into God's hands.[143]

When I think "I" is the center
Of my identity,
That I know what I need,

I eventually feel unmoored,
Frantically panicked,
Unable to breathe;

Which brings me up short
Remembering what's important:
That breath is a gift.

143. Ibid., Hebrews 10:31.

VII

Seeing myself in the context
Of Jesus' life and death
Restores me to deep peace.

He always points to his Father,[144]
The transcendent Author
Of the story his life tells:

That dependence on Source—
Not thinking he can force
Divine energy to obey him—[145]

Is definitive of who he is.
So my relationship with God
Is at the heart of who I am.

Yes, I need to become me,
Even if rebelliously,
To choose freely how to live.

That choice is what's mine,
Mine alone to make:
What is my ethic?

It takes much humility
To live relationally
With God and other people:

To call out the truth,
Protest abuse,
Live in equality,

See God in everyone,
Seek power over no one,
Be willing to suffer pain.

---

144. Ibid., Luke 2:49; 5:43; 14:7; John 15:15.
145. Ibid., Luke 4:9–12.

We read in the Psalms
God suffers long,
Along with us.[146]

In written or lived word,
It's a vulnerable God
Who lives 'mongst and within us;

Who gets pinned by Jacob,[147]
Who's defied or forgotten,
Whose heart is broken;

Who resists the temptation,
As expressed by Hosea,
To angrily destroy us.[148]

This God dwells with us,
Does not reign over us,
Continually invites us

To come follow him,
To let him teach us
Who God really is:

That "it's not by might,
Nor by power,
But by my Spirit,

Says the Lord of Hosts."[149]
He changes human hearts,
Is alive in them,

Is born as an infant,
Depends on women
And humble men

    146. Ibid., Exodus 34:6–7; Psalm 86:15.
    147. Ibid., Genesis 32:24–25.
    148. Ibid., Hosea 11:1–9.
    149. Ibid., Zechariah 4:6.

To nurture that life,
To show us how to live
As compassionate beings,

To do justice, love
Mercy, walk humbly
With Life-Source.[150]

To bring down the mighty
From their thrones[151]
With just words alone,

To put a chill in those hearts
With the truth that imparts
That their vaunted power is vain.

So too inside us—
Inside each one of us
Our pride can give way

To divine sway
Which we partner with
Day by day.

That's who God is:
A vital life force
Who breaks up the old,

So new life can live,
Even break through a crack
In impervious concrete,

Helps one make a new start
After a broken heart:
God helps one move on.

---

150. Ibid., Micah 6:8.
151. Ibid. Luke 1:46–55.

VIII

But what about death?
Even if I get the rest,
How does that fit?

Destruction and death
Are differently experienced
Depending where one stands.

We have this treasure—
This life we're given—
In earthen vessels,

In order to remind us
That the transcendent power
Belongs to God and not us.

So when facing death,
After a life of witness,
We can surrender

As Jesus did:
"Into your hands, Father,
I commend my spirit."[152]

It can seem just the end,
That nothing remains.
The person is gone.

True, the body is gone—
As well as the mind—
That form of life.

But if one believes
That there's also spirit,
That life comes from Life,

---

152. Ibid., Luke 23:46.

That Source takes human form
Of a woman is born,
Lives a human life,

That the essence is Spirit,
The self is not ultimate,
Then death is mere exit,

The end of one life,
The door to another world,
A return to the Source.

We humans can believe
There's more than what one sees:
There's imagination.

The human mind is limited,
But it can apprehend
What it can't comprehend.[153]

Imagination and words
Can bridge these two worlds,
Construct powerful symbols.

The gospel writer John
Breaks exciting new ground
Calling Jesus "the Word."[154]

This notion in his day
Would have been blasphemy,
To suggest that a human being

Is actually God's Word—
That his life and his words
Are the very voice of God;

---

153. Guite, Malcolm, *Faith, Hope, and Poetry: Theology and the Poetic Imagination*. Surrey, England: Ashgate Publishing Co., 2010, pp. 56–58.

154. The Holy Bible, John 1:1–17.

That a human being
Can manifest God;
That God is in humans,

That a human can be a Word
Bridging the worlds,
A spokesperson of God.

VIII

My Dad was one of twelve:
What chance did he have
Of having something just his?

Any pain that he had,
Any rage as a kid,
He would have buried

Just to function.
No pleasure principle,
Reality was invincible.

But he did have his Dad,
Who had a love of God,
And prayerful spirituality,

Which he passed on to me,
Which helps me to see
Beyond only me.

We are human beings
With a whole self to manage,
Lots of feelings and needs,

Which especially as children
We don't have the resources
To moderate or tolerate.

Repression comes in handy,
Helps kids wake up each morning
As if it's a new day.

But those feelings we've banked,
Deposit after deposit,
Come back to haunt us.

It's usually our own kids
Who remind us what is
Repressed deep inside.

Dad's pain was revived
Over what he'd been deprived
Of when he was a child.

My symbiotic action
Triggered his reaction
Because he sought traction

For his also nascent
Efforts to individuate,
To become a separate self.

He'd had to sacrifice too early—
When he was just a baby—
Any healthy entitlement.

He was still working that out,
Still vulnerable about
Having something just his.

This early-instilled doubt
Was too harsh no doubt,
But held an irony:

That as painful as it was,
It did help him learn
About spirituality,

In which relating to God
Involves giving up one's pride,
The self's ultimacy.

This doubt when worked out
In the crucible of love
Becomes humility.

Such spiritual growth
Accepts divine and human both
As real parts of me.

Being a man of God
Did help my Dad
Become less harsh with me.

Which in turn has helped me,
Through a long painful journey,
Let the divine gain ascendancy:

First forgive my Dad,
Because the same rage he had
Was present in me.

It's an ongoing process
Of burning away the dross
Of ego wanting ultimacy.

It's hard to carry one's cross—
To accept suffering and loss—
With spiritual maturity.

To suffer and learn
That there's joy to be had
In giving up all for God.

One then gets All back,
Lives each day in awe:
What's mine is God's All.

Life is not without pain.
And trying to place blame
Won't make pain go away.

Life's filled with pain and loss;
One lives with it best
Not inflicting it on others.

God breaks the violent cycle
By God making God's self vulnerable:
Jesus accepts the cross.

He's not a passive victim:
Sets his face towards Jerusalem,[155]
Although it leads to his death.

There's unshakable strength
In aligning oneself
With the ways of God.

Even if it means death.
That's life with depth,
Eternal life with depth.

So we too can struggle
To live Jesus' example
Of not retaliating,

To not act in anger,
Instead choose to suffer,
And thus let God speak

Of a power that seems weak
But cuts to the quick
And changes human hearts.

---

155. Ibid., Luke 9:51–54; Matthew 17:22–23; Mark 8:31–33.

IX

My Dad cried out,
He didn't strike out,
Which helped him hold back.

My Dad's angry cry
Helped him break free
Of destructive anger.

So too with me
I'm learning to be
With the pain 'neath the anger,

To suffer and endure,
To experience the courage
Of not resorting to violence.

My Dad not hitting me
Began to set us both free
To love sacrificially,

To suffer the pain,
Endure the loss,
Not pass it along,

Not escalate
Nor fuel the hate,
Further alienate.

All of this is hard,
Hard to do without God:
Be angry but sin not.[156]

One needn't be masochistic
To suffer the pain;
One can still feel outrage;

---

156. Ibid., Ephesians 4:26.

But transform that energy
Into spiritual integrity
By being with the pain,

And utter a cry,
Even a curse,
But not make things worse.

God spoke through Hosea
Words that still amaze:
How love transforms anger:

"My heart recoils within me,
My compassion grows warm and tender;
I will not execute my fierce anger.

I will not again destroy,
For I am God and no mortal,
The Holy One in your midst,

And I will not come in wrath."[157]
Here's a vulnerable God
Trusting suffering love as power,
Transforming the world.

---

157. Ibid., Hosea 11:8c–9.

Broken Ankle, Touched, and Healed

While hiking on snow-covered ice
On a slightly downward slope,
My left foot suddenly slipped out,
Then quickly caught and stopped;

But my whole body had dropped,
My rear too-tightly jammed up
Against the back of that booted foot,
My knee straight up near my chin,

And in my ankle I heard a tiny pop.
But being in a sort of shock,
I immediately dismissed the thought
That my ankle could be broken.

Carefully, I stood up, but pain shot
From my ankle up my leg to my brain.
I knew then that this was not nothing,
And looked up ahead to my companion.

She had turned, asked what happened,
But she saw from the look on my face,
And I saw reflected from her face,
The degree of pain I was in.

I cautiously leaned on the ankle
To see if it could sustain my weight.
The pain made me wince and hobble
The quarter-mile home that remained.

I continued to believe through the night
That it was nothing more than a sprain.
If only I could just get some crutches
I could get around by myself again.

Next morning I phoned the Rescue Squad,
Where a woman calm and savvy answered.
When I asked her if they rented crutches,
She made clear it was x-rays I needed.

Very early that Sunday morning
In the hospital emergency room,
The nurse was efficient and calm
As we filled out the Admission Form.

Moments later I was lying on a gurney,
Being wheeled to the x-ray room.
The technician was careful not to hurt me,
But I heard him tell someone, "It's broken."

I cursed to myself inwardly, "Damn!"
But honestly I felt some relief;
I needed to find out the truth
Before any healing could begin.

Wheeled next to a consultation room,
I sat gurney-side waiting for a doctor.
The dull ache had morphed into pain,
Filtering reality like transparency paper.

Un-officiously a woman walked in,
Dressed casually 'neath an open white coat:
Introducing herself warmly as the doctor,
She asked if I was feeling any pain.

She pointed to the boots in the room,
And asked if I'd walked in wearing them.
Though I noticed her compassionate bearing,
I interpreted that I'd done something wrong.

Ashamed, like a little boy I said , "Yes."
But she touched my knee saying, "Brave man."
My pain went cowering to the corners,
And by her touch I'm still feeling blessed!

I don't remember much else she said;
My tibia at the ankle was fractured.
Though a minor break, a cast I would need,
And follow-up with an Orthopedic doctor.

This encounter took maybe five minutes,
But the three seconds she took to touch my knee
Have stayed with me for three years and counting,
Giving new meaning to what Healing means.

From self-criticism her words released me,
And highlighted my inner resources.
Allying with the healing Spirit within,
Her touch activated powerful forces.

That woman knew a lot about healing,
Which she conveyed in an understated way.
I could tell by her manner and demeanor
That she wasn't focused on her ego or power.

She didn't think she owned healing power,
Rather, wanted to make a connection,
In which she was an agent of healing
Serving a process much greater than her.

All of that was expressed in her touch,
And actually in that moment I was healed.
It took my ankle the normal time it takes:
Four to six weeks to physically heal.

A male nurse then put on a cast,
And sure enough, there I got crutches.
Back home, I found a good Orthopedist
To assist the physical healing process.

All this helped me understand healing,
And certain Bible stories, in a new way:
There are multiple layers of healing,
Made clear to me by her touch that day.

The Lord sent Elijah to Zerephath
To a widow and son desperate for food;
He assured her that the Lord had promised
They'd have enough until the famine ended. [158]

Her meager supply of oil and meal,
From which she made cakes several days,
Was somehow, we read, not diminished,
Which left the widow truly amazed.

It's very easy to narrow one's focus
To the unfailing oil and meal.
That is indeed a part of the miracle,
But even more than that it's a metaphor

For an even deeper kind of feeding:
For the life-giving mutual nurture
That grew out of their trust in each other
And belief in the Lord's providing.

When we keep in mind miracle as metaphor,
We're ready for the rest of the story:
The severity of the widow's son's illness
Left him breathless and seemingly dead.[159]

What Elijah did next seems quite strange
To our scientific medical minds:
He took the child from his mother's bosom,
And carried him to Elijah's own bed.

He stretched himself on the child three times,
Crying O Lord, let this child live again!
Conveying that Life's Source is not one's mother,
But relationship with God's breath instead.

---

158. The Holy Bible (NRSV), 1 Kings 17:8–16.
159. Ibid., 17:17.

We read that the child revived!
The Lord listened to Elijah's prayer![160]
But let's let ourselves be surprised:
Physical contact accompanied prayer.

It's tempting to focus only on the revival,
And miss that it's through physical contact—
While knowing God is the Source of all life—
That the boy is revived and gets life back.

When the body needs to heal,
It helps to touch the body!
Physical touch is thus a symbol
That healing is also relational:

Relationships with self and another,
But there's yet an additional layer:
One's relationship with divine Spirit,
Which one accesses through worship and prayer.

Creator God lives in our bodies;
The Word is God, then becomes flesh.
The Word as embodied in Jesus
Reveals the truth about existence.

Creator God from dust forms our bodies,
Then enlivens those bodies by Spirit.
Into our nostrils god breathes Spirit breath,
And that's the deepest layer of existence.

Perhaps the pressure of Elijah's body
Three times on the widow's son's chest,
Like cardiopulmonary resuscitation,
Highlights the miracle of Life in each breath.

---

160. Ibid., 17:19–24.

From the widow's broken trust in Elijah,
And doubt about the relevance of God,
She now says, Your talk about God is Truth:
And God is speaking through your mouth.[161]

Healing's essence is restored relationship
With the Lord as Giver of life and breath;
Our bodies are designed to physically heal,
But God is with us even in death.

When Jesus heals through word or touch,
It's in order to demonstrate
That God's Spirit is present in us,
And we're whole when we live in that faith.

Jesus "was amazed at [people's] unbelief,"
At their seeing him as only a local man;[162]
They wouldn't see in him, nor in themselves,
The powerful healing Spirit of God.

The healing of the hemorrhagic woman[163]
Makes clear the healing power of touch,
By narrating that the healing happens
Without Jesus' conscious awareness.

Touch is the only initial contact she makes;
There are no words from Jesus to her.
She believes the Spirit she sees in Jesus
Is what she needs in order to be whole.

It's that Spirit that she makes contact with,
Not the conscious man Jesus himself;
But she saw it enlivening him,
And she wanted some of that for herself.

---

161. Ibid., 17:23-24.
162. Ibid., Mark 6:4-6.
163. Ibid., 5:25-34.

In the crowd she came up behind him,
Thinking to herself as she touched his cloak,
"If I [just] touch his clothes I'll be made well."[164]
And immediately her hemorrhage stopped.

It's significant that she used the passive voice;
"I'll be made well" implies an external force.
She'd endured much under many physicians,
And hadn't gotten better but worse.[165]

She sees the source of healing as outside her,
Thinks she can draw from Jesus whatever he's got.
She thus minimizes the initiative within her,
And doesn't understand the "relationships" part.

But Jesus sensed that something has happened;
He's aware that power has gone forth.[166]
It's clear it didn't happen by his exertion,
But that's not what led him to stop.

The story thus shows the power is not his:
This power is something separate from him;
But it's not an energy that can simply be taken,
So he stops and asks who has touched him.[167]

The woman wouldn't have had to admit it,
But in fear and trembling she tells the whole truth;[168]
She might have been afraid he would scold her,
But maybe also sensed something was incomplete.

Something awesome had just happened to her:
She'd made contact with divine healing power!
She could conceivably have gone away unknown,
But something this momentous merits a . . . poem.

   164. Ibid., 5:28.
   165. Ibid., 5:26.
   166. Ibid., 5:30.
   167. Ibid.
   168. Ibid., 5:33.

Jesus intention was in no way to scold her;
Just listen to what he accentuates:
"Daughter, your faith has made you well."[169]
He completes her healing by affirming her faith.

Her own faith he wanted to affirm;
Not just connecting to power outside of her.
Her inner belief that she would be healed
Revealed her inner connection to spiritual power

Already inside her, and out of that she acted;
And she knew she wanted physical contact.
Out of low self-esteem she went behind his back;
But Jesus' valuing her also healed her of that.

Jesus' parting words at first seem redundant.
He's already said, "Your faith has made you well."[170]
Then: "Go in peace, and be healed of your disease."[171]
He's distinguishing between physical and spiritual!

He first affirms her faith, then mentions her disease:
Both spiritual and physical are aspects of healing;
And the autonomy of Spirit is made clear in the touch.
What a thrill to have received Jesus' blessing!

Thus, healing is about physical healing, indeed;
That manifests how God made the world:
An inherent inclination towards physical healing;
It's not obvious that healing can also be spiritual.

Healing is evidence of divine creativity,
And "miracle" calls our attention to that power.
Even when physical or emotional healing doesn't happen,
It's God being alive within us that really matters.

---

169. Ibid., 5:34.
170. Ibid., 5:34a.
171. Ibid., 5:34b.

When someone serves a power greater than herself,
When we're touched by that person, literally or verbally,
We're reminded that that power also lives in us,
And that presence saves us from alienation and anxiety.

I was healed immediately through that humble doctor's touch,
Which physically awakened my awareness of God.
I too felt blessed, could go my way in peace,
Trusting and joining in God's healing process.

Emptiness

You want to de-clutter your life,
But you never quite get around to it.
Is the reason that you don't do it
Your fear of an emptiness inside?
The clutter is good insulation
From an internal, unsettling fear;
You don't clearly know that it's there,
But you can't make the clutter disappear.

It's hard to even imagine
The emptiness as a good thing,
To rather than fill it by eating,
You could let it be, let it be,
And listen;
To trust that your inner ear will hear
Who you are when you are raw,
And then you'll know what to do.

You can expect that
You'll be tempted to fill
That internal space
With some
Sort of substance.
The hole
Inside you
Is scary.
The vacuum
Leaves you craving
Something soothing.
But let it be, let it be
If you can.
You can.

Breathe, breathe,
I can tell you.
You will be all right.
Remember that:
You will be all right.

In fact, the emptiness
Opens you up to feel,
To feel your self breathe.
You—your "you"—
Has room to be there.
Breathe,
Deeply breathe.
You will begin to
Inhabit that space.
You are there,
"You" is there.

You can feel your life,
Being alive.
Feel your
Diaphragm move.

The beat, the beat
The very subtle
Thump
Of your heart.

You can relax, relax,
Feel yourself live;
Realize
Being alive,
Keeping yourself alive
Is not
Up to you.

In the space
Of this inner place,
Feel yourself breathe,
Breathe.
Feel yourself
Live, alive.
Contemplate
In this context
Your next move.

Let it emerge
From within,
Rather than react
Out of fear
Or to please
Or appease
Someone else.

Be
    your
        self.
Let
    Self
        Be you.

Invite
    Divine
        Self
To
    live
        you.

It's all up to you.
Yet it's not
All up to you.
You do get to choose
Whether or not
To live

As if
It's all up to you.

If you think it is
All up to you,
You'll be—
When not distracted—
Achingly alone.
An anxious person,
Inwardly restless,
Heart working hard;
You might even
Get a lot done,
But never have peace,
Always on to the next.

I don't mean to preach.
I tell myself all this too.
I have to remember
I have to come-to.

Whether by choice
Or by circumstance,
This is most truly true:
"Verily, verily,
I say unto you":
"Blessed are those
Who hunger and thirst
For righteousness,
For they will be filled."[172]
"Do not be anxious
About tomorrow."[173]
"Give us this day
Our daily bread."[174]

    172. The Holy Bible (NRSV), Matthew 5:6.
    173. The Holy Bible (RSV), Matthew 6:34a.
    174. Ibid., 6:11.

"Seek first
His kingdom,
And his righteousness."[175]
"Do not worry
About tomorrow."[176]

These words, those words,
They center me,
Re-orient me,
Are deeply calming.
Their deep authority
Always orients me.

I don't mean to preach.
Words such as these
Will often occur to me
After, after doing therapy,
Once a patient leaves,
While I'm still pondering,
What happened
Inside him or her,
Between her or him
And me.

Things come together more clearly
Sometimes
After she or he leaves.
Such words as these
Spoken by Jesus
I rarely actually say.

But that kingdom
Is at hand:[177]
That energy, that reality
Is in the air

    175. Ibid., 6:33.
    176. Ibid. (NRSV), 6:34a.
    177. Ibid. (RSV), 3:2.

That we breathe,
Breathing me.
The kingdom is near.
It's the amniotic
Atmosphere
In which the patient and I
Are swimming,
Being,
Becoming,
Healing.

"Being" Itself
Is being there
With us,
Breathing:
Ruach, wind
Is moving,
Animating us:
Spirit Wind
In you and me.

Oh, there's still mess,
Oh, there's still death.
Growing pains don't end,
Things turned on end.
Ego dies hard,
Digs in its heels,
Gasps for its life;
Grasps for control,
Might even start a war
In an effort not to see
The shadow in me.
My ego would rather see
In the other
The demon in me.

I don't mean to preach.
Much of this I don't say;
But it's the air that I breathe,
The Spirit that breathes me.
So we're affected anyway,
The patient and me.
We're changed mysteriously
By this Word being me,
By the half-thought-out words
I do manage to say,
By the underlying love
Which in healing comes to play.

I feel moving in me
From a source deep below,
A Source so vast and deep
That it threatens to blow
Away the frail but necessary
Self-restraint that I need
So that the patient can grow
At the pace she or he needs.

The roiling and relieving
Inner-earth heaving and
Simultaneous placidity:
The scalding lava
Of cleansing tears,
The ocean-size inner
Aquifer of love
Threatens
To blast up
Through the well
That my patient and I
Have carefully drilled
Patiently, layer by layer
Down into his or her identity
In the course of being healed.

It's a so-much-more[178]
Than imaginable
Transformation
That one can barely contain it.
But it's this very same love
That helps me be serene,
To regulate the uptake
Dose by tolerable dose
So as not
To overwhelm
The patient's ego
Or my own.

It's an awesome
Thrilling thing,
A pulsing tingling
Throughout my body:
A quickened breathing,
A healing love
Barely bounded
By my skin—
This love
We're swimming in.

Our bodies are
The material base
For the alchemy
Of love,
For the energy
That moves,
Lives,
Not body-bound,
But willing to indwell
My patient and me.

---

178. Ibid. (NRSV), Romans 5.

Each of us
Is changed
In this intimate
Exchange,
Becoming
More known
To ourselves
And each other.
Able to part
When ripened—
Though each of us
Will mourn—
Because of
The healing connection
To Spirit between
And within.

We may start with rage
Or shuttered numbness,
So as not to feel our pain.
Then in the crucible
Of healing
We feel it again
And cannot remain
The same person
We used to be.

Pouring out our pain,
We feel it again,
But this time it's gain,
Due to compassion.
The pain's not in vain,
Because this time we stand
With the Healer outside
And increasingly within.
The recurring pain
Will no longer define us,

Nor give us our name.
We're more than our wound
Or recurrent shame,
Free to respond
Differently,
We're reborn.

There's a lot deep inside
I wanna keep packed away;
Stuff I can no longer hide
When I become empty.
How we fear,
How we fear
That first step
We need to take
If we're gonna
Grow
Spiritually.

It's in the emptiness
That I can become
Aware of being full;
Discovering that
There's more
To me
Than my ego.

Jesus in humility
Didn't regard equality
With divinity
As something to use
Manipulatively,
But emptied himself
To be born of a woman
In human form,
To the point of death
Even death on a cross.

Therefore God
Exalted him.[179]

When we're
Heard and seen
In good therapy,
We gradually
Begin to see
Through becoming
Open and empty
Who we're
Spiritually
Meant to be:
"Being" being me.

---

179. Ibid. (RSV), Philippians 2:6–9.

Benjy Suffers Life, and Is There a Point?

I'd read William Faulkner's The Sound and the Fury twice;
Then shortly after the second time I had the chance,
To attend a production[180] of that part of the story
Told from the viewpoint of developmentally disabled Benjy.

Before seeing the Play, I'd wondered how they'd present it,
And how do so in a way that would add anything to it
Not gotten from the mesmerizing experience of reading it.
I left the theatre stunned at the power previously latent.

Drawn into the drama at at least three different levels,
I saw, heard, and felt the quick evasive maneuvers
Used by the family members to avoid any real contact;
Decibel levels rose whenever any two might connect.

The cacophony of siblings simultaneously talking
At each other, past each other, and over each other loudly,
Their sick mother alternately whining and demanding,
Was at one level funny, but more fundamentally empty.

In the midst of all this is three to thirty year old Benjy,[181]
So developmentally disabled that he can't even talk;
But he communicated so well as to leave me in shock
Every time he was shoved or his hat was knocked off.

In the family's daily life, the father was mostly gone,
While the mother floated 'round ghostly in just a nightgown,
Indefinably sickly but refinedly manipulative,
Leaving Benjy, his brothers and sister, emotionally deprived.

    180. A presentation by (New York Theatre Workshop) Elevator Repair Service on May 30, 2008.
    181. The names "Benjy" and "Ben" refer to the same person throughout the poem; Faulkner writes about him at different ages.

II

The social structure with slavery had been taken apart,
Along with the fraudulent Christianity that sustained it;
Thus revealing that enslavement rots most the heart
Of the slaveholders, and leaves them spiritually decadent.

There's nothing in scripture on which to base such a structure;
The whole thrust of the Exodus is God setting people free.
The dynamic of domination leaves the Dominator less secure;
Major resources must be devoted to maintaining security.

A slaveholder by definition becomes increasingly inhuman,
Not just in mistreating others, but even more internally.
One has to lie to oneself that one is better than common,
Thus denying the reality of one's existential dependency.

This dependency then into the slave gets projected,
Who's dependent on the master for every human need.
This all gets supported by contorted rationalizations
Which leave the master feeling powerful and thinking he's free.

But by denying his dependency and his core need for love—
Which one can only receive in vulnerability—
He tries to coerce love, but thus never can trust
That any caring he gets is truly loving and free.

An inner emptiness grows, a longing and aching,
Which cannot be filled by whatever one's taking.
The alcohol one drinks in hopes of its slaking
A raw stomach's thirst, becomes one's unmaking.

All this can't be acknowledged: that would be weak;
Instead it's acted out, and by each differently.
Benjy's father's an alcoholic, his mother's always sick;
Estrangement between them scrambles sexuality.

It's energies fly around, neither held nor shaped by love,
Reducing one to base instincts or graspings for love.

The South idealized white women as almost pure beyond touch,
While raping black women, though not calling it such.

This Madonna/whore split –here between white and black,
Reflected and reinforced sex being split off from love;
When a Master didn't act out, instead, held himself back,
His desire would build up and make him afraid of contact.

But the absence of love leaves one never at peace:
Estranged from oneself and afraid of intimacy;
One grows increasingly cold to oneself and to others,
Becoming a dead person walking or behaving brutally.

III

These various ways of coping are captured by Faulkner
In the various characters he creates so realistically,
That whether you identify with one or feel appalled by another,
You begin to see in yourself what you formerly couldn't see.

Benjy's older brother Quentin is sent off to Harvard,
But he can't date nor study because he's so preoccupied
With longings for his sister Caddy, whom he's idealized,
That when she behaves promiscuously, he commits suicide.

She'd become pregnant out of wedlock, and when Quentin found out,
He'd confronted and fought the man but was soundly defeated.
For Quentin's sake Caddy agreed never again to speak to the lout,
But then alone and with child she married a man she'd deceived.

When her husband found out that it wasn't his child,
He sent Caddy and her daughter away in disgrace.
When Quentin had first found out that Caddy was with child,
He'd tried to take on the blame by saying it was incest.

When parents aren't loving, siblings might turn to each other
For the comfort and connection that every human needs:

Lack of parental affirmation prevents inner psychic structure,
Making it difficult for each sibling to separate and leave.

Caddy herself was a lively, adventurous character.
Her parents' scrambled sexuality seemed to gather in her.
As a prepubescent girl her brothers saw her muddy knickers
When she climbed a tree to a window to view their dead
  grandmother.

The sexual energy she carried was hard to contain,
Especially given the family background and her longing to be
  known.
Her energies did get her launched beyond the family domain,
But betrayal, death, and heartache drove her far away from home.

The most chilling of the siblings, disconnected from emotion,
Is Jason the Fourth, the third child of four,
Who takes responsibility for the family's financial situation,
Which someone had to do, but he misused his power.

Once the father had died the family structure grew weaker,
The South's socio-economic changes were harder to ignore;
They kept the vestiges of slavery by keeping black servants,
But the survivors of that era were hard for Jason to support.

Jason became in bold relief the perverse sort of person
Who's the product of a social system built around greed;
Where the ultimate value is material acquisition
At the expense of compassion and helping those in need.

He was also the favorite child of his mother,
Which bonded him to her and made it hard for him to leave;
But he grew increasingly bitter over taking care of the others,
And grew increasingly cold over no one meeting his needs.

He resented his sister Caddy, who in her own way broke free,
And Quentin going to college only to waste it all in death.
Saddled with the care of his mother, his niece, and Benjy,
His bitterness grew until he had no heart left.

Jason's niece is Miss Quentin, daughter of Caddy,
Who lives with the family after Caddy went away.
In cold-hearted greed Jason blackmails sister Caddy
Into his being Quentin's Guardian, then steals her support pay.

But Miss Quentin came to know that money was Jason's weakness.
Uncannily children know what adults try to hide.
Teenagers—even children—ferret out family secrets;
She found the money he'd been stealing and went on the run.

Jason violently raged when he found what she'd done.
This cache of money he'd embezzled was what he'd lived for.
He stormed off to get the sheriff to pursue Miss Quentin;
But the sheriff knew the story, so Jason lost his power.

Finding meaning in money became increasingly bankrupt;
His efforts to make things right fell apart one by one.
But this further loss of meaning made him even more dangerous;
Only cold-hearted anger kept him from being totally undone.

IV

The other household members are the African American servants,
Whose position on the face of it echoes the time of slavery:
They're intimately involved in the life and care of the family,
Economically still dependent though spiritually free.

Grandma Dilsey the matriarch has been through it all:
From slavery in the Compson family to legal liberty.
Her deep abiding Faith make her both free and loyal,
Her presence and power survive the worst that can be.

The most moving part of the book is the fourth and last chapter,
In which Dilsey goes to church walking alongside of Benjy.
No way she's gonna miss attending worship on Easter;
Come on, she says, we're not waiting for Luster or Frony.

"Dey kin ketch up wid us," she said, "We gwine hear de singin.'"
Benjy was wailing on quietly about her scolding of Luster.
Frony and Luster caught up, and Dilsey said to Ben "Now den,"
And Ben ceased his wailing as they talked about the preacher.[182]

They pass groups of white people going to a church of their own;
Daughter Frony disapproves of Dilsey bringing Ben along.
She says her discomfort is due to what other folks are saying,
But Dilsey cuts through the prejudice to say God isn't minding.

As they get nearer the church, children call Ben a Loony,
But the person we're focused on is the unflappable Dilsey.
She chooses whom she'll speak to; otherwise lets Frony
Respond to all greeters rather than address them directly.

Faulkner's artistry is amazing as the church scene unfolds;
He makes clear through the dialogue just what Dilsey seeks:
That though she "ain't feelin' well," what the church service holds
Is "De comfort and de unburdenin'" that her weary heart needs.

When their minister appeared with his highly touted guest,
He looked so insignificant that the people were astonished.
When he stood up to speak, he sounded like a white man;
They were curious but doubtful that they'd be impressed.

Then suddenly his voice altered from its former white tone,
Took on a resonant "sad timbrous quality like an alto horn,"
Which "sank into their hearts" and "spoke there again":
"I got the recollection and the blood of the Lamb."

This "undersized, wizened, insignificant"-looking man,
"Whose body fed the voice that had fleshed its teeth in him,"
Began to speak in their idiom, "Breddren en sistuhn,"
"Is you got de ricklickshun en de blood of de Lamb?"

---

182. Quotation marks indicate verbatim quotes from William Faulkner, *The Sound and the Fury*. New York: Random House, 1929, the fourth and last chapter, entitled "April Eighth 1928," pp. 206–49.

The voice "continued and consumed him until he was nothing,
Until they all were nothing and there was not even a voice;
Instead they felt their hearts speaking one to another
In chanting measures beyond the need [any more] for words."

"Dilsey sat there bolt upright", her hand on Ben's knee;
"Two tears slid down" her face as the Preacher did preach.
Her face bore the marks of "myriad coruscations,"
Left by years of "immolation" and renunciation.

The Preacher went on preaching the terms of salvation,
How God won't load down heaven with everyone who comes.
God will turn away his face if there's no ricklickshun
Of the agony he suffers over people killing his Son.

In the weeping and the wailing of women's lamentations,
The Preacher hears the weepin' of God's turnt-away face;
He sees the darkness and death of everlastin' generations,
But he sees in Jesus' death, that God is with us in darkness.

But the Preacher doesn't stop there: the story goes on;
Beyond darkness he sees light in Jesus' resurrection.
The meaning in Jesus' death is that death is not the end:
This human story we know is only part of a larger one.

Amidst the preaching and responses, Ben was not wailing;
Midst all this he sat rapt in his "sweet blue-eyed gaze."
Beside him sat Dilsey, "bolt upright and crying,"
Healed and annealed while someone sang, "I sees Jesus!"

As they began walking home, Ben nor Dilsey made a sound,
Dilsey's "tears took their sunken and devious courses";
Frony rebuked Dilsey's crying with white folks around;
Dilsey said, "Never you mind, I've seed de first en de last."

Frony still didn't get it, and asked, "First en last whut?"
Wouldn't allow herself to look inward nor under the surface;
She was still viewing herself through the eyes of the white world,
Revealing the damage slavery does to one's freedom of spirit.

Dilsey does dry her eyes before reaching the street,
Adapting to the white world, but with core identity intact.
Ben shambles along beside her, watching Luster's cocky anticks,
But begins whimpering again when their rotting house he sees.

From this time of deep connection with Spirit and heart,
They stand looking at their house with its "rotting portico";
Thus returning to daily life and the family falling apart,
Dilsey resumes her servant role and picks up the mother's fallen
   Bible.

The artistry of Faulkner is to make his theology implicit;
So much so that one could say, "What? There's no theology!"
Especially since the novel's title gives Shakespeare the credit,
Where the phrase "signifying nothing" follows "full of sound and
   fury."

Faulkner does write explicitly that Ben's "bellowing abjectly"
Is "the grave hopeless sound of all voiceless misery under the sun."
But he also makes clear through the Preacher and Dilsey
That God suffers with us and that Ben is "de Lawd's chile/ [son]."

The power of the book, what makes it haunting and profound,
Is that God is present in the worst of life, in silence and sound;
Such that even when there's "nothing," God's loving heart beats,
And the transcendent symbol is a "serene tortured crucifix."

V

For some more of the worst of it, we must return to Jason,
Who after their mother died, had Benjy put in the asylum.
Secretly before that, he'd had himself made Benjy's Guardian,
And without their mother's knowledge he'd had Ben castrated.

Ben had played in the back yard, contained by a fence;
On the other side of it a road, golf course in the distance.
Teen girls walked to school each day down that road,
And Ben's guttural gropings were as scary as words.

School and town were alarmed, demanded some action.
And the next thing we know, Ben is standing there castrated!
As mentioned before, the family didn't deal well with sex,
And especially son Jason had become cruel and heartless.

As enacted in the Play, Ben stands alone center-stage,
Facing the audience with horror and shock on his face;
His arms are stretched out, he's looking down at his groin,
Howling via a chorus "They're gone, they're gone, they're gone."

I sat there in my seat, laid out like dead weight,
So flattened with horror I couldn't integrate
That one human being could do this to another;
That Jason could do this to Ben his own brother.

Jason's other chilling actions, at the end of the play,
Are the firing of the servants, and having Ben sent away.
It's a heart-breaking scene: Ben standing at the door;
Their mother has died, there's no family left any more.

It's quite easy to hate Jason, to see him as the villain;
But it's no accident that Faulkner gives him lots of attention.
After all, he is dealing with a society's disintegration;
His cruelty and his greed are driven largely by desperation.

His loss is unspoken, maybe too great to bear,
So he cuts off his emotions, except for brutal anger.
He isolates himself, seeking money, control, and power;
And in his own violent way, he tries to recreate order.

VI

The title of the book is The Sound and the Fury;
The violence and the wailing are prevalent throughout.
These two themes are incarnate in Jason and Benjy.
But what could calm these two men is what the book is about.

When I left the theater that evening, I couldn't talk either;
Like Ben, I was dumb, and like Dilsey, quietly crying.
Ben's suffering touched me deeply, but I didn't get until later
That Ben lives a layer of life that antecedes speaking.

I too felt neutered, beleaguered, and empty.
I understood why Ben wailed as if life's a lost cause.
He was helpless as a baby and at people's mercy:
But he did have that wail and his longing for love.

What dawned on me later was that Ben's preverbal existence,
No matter how old he was chronologically,
Captured that level of universal human experience
Of how sensitive we are and how cruel life can be.

At least he could wail to protest mistreatment,
And his wail pierced even the hardest of hearts,
Most often eliciting efforts from others to relieve it,
Though Luster provokes him to get the wailing started.

Perhaps Luster did this to express his own pain:
As a young man himself he had to take care of Ben.
It was a role he hadn't chosen, and again and again,
Dilsey would pull him away from doing his own thing.

The efforts to calm Ben had different derivations.
The most positive was from Caddy and arose out of love.
Others no doubt such as their mother and Jason
Had similar anguish they didn't want reminding of.

Ben was calm in the presence of the two people who loved him:
The long-suffering Dilsey and his beloved sister Caddy.
It's clear early in the story and viscerally touching
That Caddy has a heart and just simply loves Benjy.

After Caddy leaves home and Ben is much older,
He'll sometimes be calm while holding her old shoe;
But he longs for her presence and never really gets over
The loss of her, made worse by golfers calling "caddy" too.

Ben would also calm down when staring at fire.
In a primitive way he seemed to see mystery,
Be enchanted by the transforming aspect of fire:
It was burning things up but gave life-giving heat.

Fire burned away distractions, compelling Ben's focus:
Perhaps the alchemical process captured his gaze:
That the mixture of suffering, love, and divine presence
Yields the deepest heart connection that all beings crave.

VII

While love was the main thing that calmed Benjy down,
The other had to do with a deep sort of order;
An order made manifest in structure and routine,
But rooted in the relationship between Creator and creature.

Benjy suffers so much and there seems to be no point;
What meaning can there be in all this loss and decay?
Life seems to have no meaning, be "a tale told by an idiot,"
Who "struts and frets" and wails "his hour upon the stage."[183]

It's only in deep order that there's any real hope;
Everything else dies in the transforming fire of change.
Time-bound structures and identities melt away like snow,
But even violence, decay, and death don't make God go away.

Once again I was awed at the artistry of Faulkner:
His symbols are subtle, and in that lies their power.
In the last story of the book this is all packed together
In Ben's ride in the surrey while holding a broken flower.

It's something Ben is used to, this weekly surrey ride,
Undertaken by Luster's uncle, Dilsey's son named T. P.
Every Sunday he takes Ben on a ride to the graveyard,
And even the ancient horse Queenie knows route and routine.

---

183. Shakespeare, William. Macbeth, Act 5, Scene 5.

This Sunday's ride's delayed because T. P. isn't yet home.
Dilsey's weary of waiting, saying, "Dis long time, O Jesus."
Luster masks opportunity in the guise of compassion:
Eagerly offering to drive Ben, and Dilsey, with warnings, agrees.

Luster had just provoked Ben, saying "Caddy, Caddy, Caddy,"
So we're doubtful of his promises to keep himself in check.
But he'd also gotten Ben a flower, and mended it cleverly,
Which Ben's holding in his fist, eyes serene and unstressed.

It's not long before Luster begins assuming a swagger
In comic disproportion to clopping horse and old surrey.
He can't resist showing off and being careless of danger:
He swings the horse off course, thus provoking Ben's fury.

Luster'd seen Jason's car, but, being full of himself,
He wanted to show off to a nearby group of Negroes.
"For an instant," Faulkner writes, Ben sat "in utter hiatus,"
Then, in "more than astonishment," he bellows and bellows.

Luster is now frantic as Ben's voice reaches crescendo;
He tries to rein in Queenie while telling Ben to hush.
Jason jumps into the surrey and deals Luster a blow,
Violently turns Queenie around as Ben's voice becomes hoarse.

Jason slashes Queenie back into the usual corridor,
And being who he is, he strikes Luster on the head.
In his violent way, he tries to re-establish order,
Then reaches back and hits Ben, breaking the flower again.

He jumps off the surrey and tells Luster to go straight home,
Threatening to kill him if he ever drives the wrong way again.
Luster does as he's told, "Git to hell [on] home with him,"
While Ben roars and roars; all efforts to quiet him are vain.

Then in the very last paragraph, Faulkner sums up the story.
It's poignant in the extreme because it captures it all.
Queenie moves on again, feet clop-clopping steadily;
Ben hushes at once as life's regular rhythm resumes:

"The broken flower drooped over Ben's fist[,] and his eyes
Were empty and blue and serene again, as cornice
And façade flowed smoothly once more from left to right;
Post and tree . . . and signboard, each in its ordered place."

VIII

Ben's holding his broken flower. Let's read that again.
Ben IS a broken flower: and what a metaphor!
We're each a broken flower, held in some cradling hand,
And whose "hand" we believe it is, will shape what we live for.

But what hope is this? We want a life free of pain!
Caught up in ourselves, we want life on our terms.
But life as we know it, right from the beginning,
Has, yes, love and joy, but also much suffering.

When we look at the face of it, love seems weaker than force,
But unselfish love reflects the heart of the Creator;
Connection to that Heart stokes an alchemical fire
That gives meaning to suffering and strength to endure.

Even Ben in the asylum, no doubt wailing, sad, alone,
Is at least held by some structure, he's not entirely on his own.
Jason, thrashing around violently, does get things done;
He's lost familiar structures, too; does he deserve compassion?

He may not deserve it; but Faulkner's all about heart,[184]
Which includes pity and love, and thus compassion.
This heart-wrenching tale of things falling apart
Invites us to think twice about our basic orientation.

---

184. By using Google or another computer Search Engine, you can access and read the brief, powerful, and touching Nobel Prize Speech of William Faulkner, in which his focus is the human spirit and the human heart. He speaks of "the old verities and truths of the heart, . . . love and honor and pity and pride and compassion and sacrifice," and he goes on to say that a human is immortal because "he [or she] has a soul, a spirit capable of compassion and sacrifice and endurance."

Faulkner's unflinching honesty about the harshness of life,
And the behavior of these characters as they try to cope,
Invites us to wail just like Benjy, and to recognize in ourselves
The Jason, Dilsey, Caddy, and Luster, seeking order and love.

The choices each makes as they respond to Ben's wailing,
Exposes who each is and how their lives will unfold.
Seeing them in ourselves, we can reconsider life's meaning,
And strive to be our best selves, which though broken, can grow.

In the end it's not a happy tale, so why read or see it?
What holds our attention—though it's hard to see or read?
For me, it's the divine heart that is present in the suffering,
Which helps me do justice, love mercy, and walk more humbly.[185]

---

185. The Holy Bible (RSV), Micah 6:8.

Quetzal at El Triunfo

In the ancient cloud forest El Triunfo,
State of Chiapas in southwestern Mexico,
Dwells an elusive primeval bird
With the strangest call hardly heard:

Having seen a photo in advance
Of this elongate bird,
I figured if it sang perchance,
It couldn't possibly not be heard.

To demonstrate the sound
Our leader opened his mouth
In the shape of a circle, then
Blew, but no sound came out.

This preparation gave me pause,
Surely shifted my momentum
From assertive birding action
To respectful patient listening.

This bird the Resplendent Quetzal
Is heard by the human ear
As a haunting background un-sound,
A sound you inversely hear,

As when lightly blowing
Over the top of a bottle,
More mute than a flute,
Like a whispering owl.

Its body-size like a large parrot
Has three-foot long tail coverts
Colored forest-green like its back feathers,
And a startling resplendent red breast.

Any hope of ever seeing it
Lies in trying to inhabit
This forest it lives in
With a reverent spirit.

With an eager open heart,
I hoped it would manifest.
I gradually began to intuit
Why Mayans thought it blessed.

Out birding at six a.m. one morning,
Barely awake with the dawning day,
The local guide started yelling,
"The Quetzal, look, look, the Quetzal!"

He was pointing up at the sky
Clear blue off in the distance.
I saw a phantom flutter by,
Like train cars following an engine.

This was such an unusual sight,
It took time for me to integrate,
That this was the Quetzal in flight
With its long tail rippling after it.

These fleeting several seconds
Will remain with me forever.
My heart still beats a little faster.
But was it an apparition?

No, other people saw it
Traveling through the sky:
How its vulnerable existence
Human souls can still inspire.

Later I saw it in the forest,
I heard its breathy unsound.
It manifested transcendence,
Hidden presence all around.

As Her Pastor

As her Pastor,
I went to visit her
In the hospital one day.

Didn't want to go,
Didn't like her;
I doubted she liked me.

She was seventy-nine,
A widow, had one son
Who lived in Hawaii.

She was crotchety,
Had exacting standards,
Told it the way she saw it.

On the face of it,
She accorded no favors
To authorities.

I'd known her for three years;
She always greeted me,
But she rarely smiled.

She'd probably have said
That liking each other
Isn't what really matters;

What matters is integrity,
Being honest and true:
A good heart.

I'd think to myself,
"A warm heart
Would go a long way, too."

I never did learn
What wounds
She was covering.

I didn't know why
She was in the hospital,
Nor how we learned of it.

So with trepidation,
I went to see her,
Expecting criticism—

Where had I been?
Why not come sooner?
It's hard to reach you.

Upon entering the room
I saw the fear in her eyes.
Past time for criticism,

Beyond setting things right
Any more in this life.
She looked terrified.

I was scared now, too,
Unprepared for this:
Hadn't known this person.

But my sense of death
In the room
And the fear in her eyes

Did help me shift gears,
Lay down my arms,
And be with her.

I could see in her eyes
For the first time
That she was glad to see me.

A door had opened here;
There was room for me
In her room.

"Not doing well," she said,
And then she coughed,
Yes, she coughed,

She'd brought her
Hand to her mouth,
Then drew it away.

Sweet Jesus help me!
I'll never forget
What lay in her hand there:

There lay these pinkish
Gray porous chunks
Of . . . her lungs!

In freeze-frame slow motion
I spent whole seconds
Taking this in.

So shocked
I'm amazed that I stayed
In the room. Thank God.

This was a situation
Where being in role
Helped me function:

Rather than turn, run,
Sick to my stomach,
Dash to the bathroom.

Everything was
Different from here on;
Terms not the same.

I knew for sure now
What was happening.
Poor vulnerable Being.

Her cough made clear to me,
And maybe to herself, too,
What was happening.

Death was definitely
Rattling us,
A daunting force.

Though outmaneuvered and
Momentarily disarmed,
I was still her Pastor.

As her Pastor
I saw her disintegration,
Shared her anguish.

She'd kept so much inside;
Couldn't any more.
She was undone.

I don't remember
What I said.
But I stayed.

The Spirit spoke
Through my presence.
"O Esther," I said.

The nurse came,
Cleaned her hand.
I held her hand.

I didn't stay long;
She was drained.
She was dying.

I said a prayer;
Saw deep love
In her eyes,

Eyes full of tears,
Heading into rest.
Still in shock, I left.

The next day
The Church Receptionist
Told me of her death.

Peace at the last?
I think so. God knows
Her Pastor had come.

It's thirty-five years hence;
I'm still trying to process
All that happened between us.

I was her Pastor.
What an honor,
What a horror!

The Spirit helps
Us do far better
Than we could muster.

The Senior Pastor
Presided at her funeral.
But a few months later

I received a Greeting Card
From her son—
Postmarked "Hawaii"—

In which he thanked me
For my kindness
To his mother!

Adding that she had often
Spoken well of me
As her "fine young Pastor."

A final shock—this blessing
That the Spirit sent me
From her through her son.

One doesn't learn this stuff
In Theological Seminary:
One can't really:

The guarded forms love takes
So as to keep intact
The ways wounded souls cope.

Hands

Huge hands:
Twice the size of mine,
His son.
Hands he used
To hit me with
When I was young.
Spanking, they called it
Back then,
On the bottom.

Farmer's hands:
Work-worn,
Rough and tough,
Thick-skinned,
Nails not
Always clean:
Cleaning machines,
Barns, pigpens;
Shoveling grain.

Raised on a farm. Then
From the age of twenty,
On a farm of his own,
Till he made the decision
At the age of forty
To move to town
To pursue his dream
Doing what he loved:
Working with wood.

When moving lumber,
He wore leather gloves

To prevent splinters
From piercing his skin
Or sliding under
His fingernails.
As lumberyard foreman,
He built and trained men
Until his retirement.

Woodworking
Was his hobby—
Actually an
Avocation—which
Matured him
Into a Craftsman,
An Artisan,
A clock-maker,
Toy creator.

His toolshed on the farm
Became a larger
Shop in the basement
When he moved
From farm to town.
Walnut became
His main medium,
With oak a
Sometime second.

Self-educated
After eighth grade,
He loved to read.
Built a solar-operated
Wood-drying shed
Of which he
Was duly proud.
Most of his wood
Cured in that shed.

Over the years,
He progressed
From rough
To refined:
From work on the farm
Building hog-houses,
Fences, wagons,
Sheds and barns,
To finer items.

Refinement
Of his identity
Was also happening:
From respected
Farmer to renowned
Artist and Craftsman,
With a growing
Professional confidence
Flowing from his hands.

Grandfather clocks,
Walnut wall clocks,
Mantel clocks,
Roll-top desks,
Lathe-turned legs
Of end tables,
Coffee tables,
Kitchen tables,
Matching chairs.

Bedroom dressers.
Glass-enclosed
China finery
Hutches with doors.
Drawers that closed
With a whisper
When barely touched.

Furniture made-to-order
From a picture.

He sold many clocks,
Much walnut furniture.
The Des Moines Register
Did a full-feature article
With photos of him at work
In his basement Wood Shop.
He built a backyard shed
To store his dried wood
Waiting to be transformed.

All this he did actually
As part of a team,
Because my mother
Did all the finishing:
First applying stain;
Then three coats
Of polyurethane;
Sanding each time
Till the wood shone.

He cut off his thumb
While planing a board.
The first joint was gone;
He found it on the floor.
Mom was at a meeting.
He waited till she got home,
Drove to an emergency room,
But nothing could be done;
He's left with half a thumb.

This didn't stop his work,
Maybe slowed him down.
They partnered for years.
Mom did complain,
Kept going just the same

Till she was almost eighty,
Had less and less energy.
Then came the toys,
Which he himself painted.

He always kept reading,
Coin and stamp collecting;
But wood would flow
Through his hands,
Handling various tools,
And take form
As from nothing
Into intricate
Creations.

At what point
Did all this consciously
Become an art?
Somewhere between
The newspaper article
And when he and Mom
Took his lifelike toys
To a nearby Craft Fair,
And people's eyes glowed.

Meanwhile, Mom
Had begun knitting
Beautifully and variably
Patterned afghans,
Which she arranged
To display and sell
At the Iowa State Fair
In Des Moines,
Where she shone.

Works of respected
And respective hands,
Guided daily

By creative brains.
Her delicate hands
Stitched huge afghans
And polished wood;
His rough hands
Formed delicate toys.

By the time they
Left the farm,
We three sons
Had left home.
Their generativity
Took artistic form.
They also had friends,
Loved their Church,
And traveled some.

Mom got hit
By a speeding car
As a pedestrian
On a rainy evening,
Was thrown
Several yards;
Her neck was broken.
In a hospital bed
She lay prone

With a head brace
Screwed into the bone
Of her skull
For a few weeks.
She wasn't supposed to move.
She tried not to laugh
About wearing bright red
Tennis shoes in bed
So her feet wouldn't drop.

Dad fell face-down
On concrete one
Columbus Day weekend
When the bottom
Of the twenty-foot
Ladder he was on
Slipped backwards and out
On slippery snow,
And he at top came crashing down,

Still clinging to the ladder.
His nose landed on a rung
And was broken.
He was out cold,
Knees and nose bleeding.
An ambulance came,
But he was soon flown,
Airlifted by helicopter,
To a hospital in Des Moines.

He was unconscious
For a couple days;
He looked so small
In bed there;
Began to come round,
But was confused.
Filled with terror,
I told him I wasn't
Ready for him to die.

With his customary
Deep-throated
Slightly amused
And confident laugh,
He immediately said,
"O, I'm not gonna die;
Not yet, anyway."

I've never felt as connected
To him as on that day.

Before that talk,
When we were all
Still uncertain
About the outcome,
My Uncle Nelson
Stood priestly facing me
And reminded me of
The spiritual ground
We all stand on.

With a voice full
Of unwavering authority,
He addressed my fear
And said, "Carroll,
As the Pastor said,
There's living grace
And there's dying grace;
Whichever one you need,
You'll be given."

I didn't know
He had it in him;
He was a quiet man.
It reminded me
Of William Faulkner
Writing of a Preacher
Whose voice
Came from beyond
And took hold of him.

From grace through Nelson
I was indeed given
Strength to tell my Dad
What I said.
Though I was shaken,

I felt something moving
In the air like a wind
Which was thrilling
And set my hair on end.

Openness to Spirit
Is a wonderful thing;
It's hard to sustain
That intense attention
For very long.
But that's fine,
Because precisely then
One can truly rest, and
Feel sustained again.

They both recovered,
Their lives went on,
Physically uncompromised,
Even strengthened,
For thirty or more years.
They welcomed, enjoyed,
And loved grandchildren,
Then great-grandchildren
Still being born.

One hot August day
On vacation in Albuquerque,
I got a call from Ken
My brother, saying
They'd been in an accident
With their Chevy S 10,
The red pickup truck
They went everywhere in.
They survived again.

Dad had made a left turn
Facing oncoming traffic
With an apparent

Lapse in attention.
An SUV hit them,
And totaled the S 10.
Somehow my Dad was
More injured than Mom,
With a blow to his head.

Once again in hospital
In serious condition,
He was now eighty-two.
Seriously shaken,
He was conscious,
But bleeding
Inside his head:
A hematoma,
Blood on the brain.

This time it
Was his skull
They drilled into:
In order to drain
The blood off his brain.
He soon returned home,
But it remained
To be ascertained
If he could drive again.

He had no doubts,
Was actually disgusted
That he had to be tested.
The doctors had to assess
Cognitive functioning.
He passed every test.
He initially insisted
It wasn't his fault,
The accident.

My brother found out,
By talking to the cops,
It was indeed his fault.
He found it hard to accept
That he'd made a mistake.
I know what that's like:
One wants to deny
The truth of such acts,
Turn back the clock.

He recovered from it all,
Resumed driving like before,
Hopefully humbled but
Not showing it at all.
My mother didn't drive,
So she was relieved;
I guess she resigned herself
To the contingency of life,
Whatever might befall.

He came back strong,
But she began to wane.
Congestive heart failure
Was the name
Given her condition.
First a pacemaker,
Then defibrillator;
But mostly her love
Kept her alive.

People were her life,
Filled her with delight.
She also kept cooking,
Baking apple pies.
At their sixtieth anniversary,
We threw a big party.
Both extended families

Came round to celebrate
Over the course of two days.

She was in her glory.
Second son Dean
Facilitated stories
Told by all attendees:
Years of memories,
Several about their courting.
Dad sat there frozen,
A private person;
Found all this embarrassing.

At about this time
We all heard from Mom:
In her resolute way
She was insisting
On a family photo,
Which Dad hated.
But he did it.
Now that she's gone,
We all treasure it.

Yes, now she's gone.
Eighty-six years old.
Twenty-fourth of August,
Two-thousand thirteen.
Hoped to die at home,
That's what Dad wanted:
Not a Nursing Home.
He didn't want to spend money
And feared being alone.

But that couldn't go on;
They couldn't cope on their own.
Finally Hospice came in
With a hospital bed.
Then to the Hospice home,

Where we all visited Mom,
Especially Dad,
Who at eighty-seven
Still gets around.

Three weeks she was there,
And a couple days more.
They combed her hair,
She couldn't any more.
There on the first weekend,
She was still coherent;
Mairead and I visited.
Saying goodbye was poignant:
I'll never forget it.

She was in a Recliner,
Asked for a drink of water.
Love boils down to that:
Giving a cup of water to her.
She sipped and leant back,
Sighed "thank you," and relaxed.
I cut up her dinner meat;
She ate all of that:
Hadn't stopped eating yet.

That day and a half
Were for me such a gift.
I can hardly write yet
What I felt as I left.
"We have to go, Mom,
Back to New York," I said.
"Back to New York?!"
In a stricken tone she said.
I choked on my words.

I knew that I'd never ever
See her alive again.
We both understood

That this was the end.
That invisible bond
And our clasping hands
Outspoke any words.
In the clutch, she said
"Thanks for all your letters."

I was taken aback,
Emotion blocking my words;
Because here she was,
Filling the word gap,
Taking the lead now
In saying final goodbyes:
Summing up in one sentence
The connective tissue
That had existed between us.

Ever since I'd left home
At seventeen, still so young,
We used letters, not phone,
As the way to stay connected.
Whether conscious or intuitive,
I see now her wisdom
In that mode of communication:
Phone would be too intimate,
Letters blessed individuation.

In my gut-twisting pain
Over this being the end,
I couldn't respond,
Till Mairead gave me the words:
Saying emphatically to Mom,
"Thank YOU for your letters!"
"Yes, thanks for all your letters
Through all of those years;
You were so faithful," I said.

The obvious remained unsaid:
That I'd never see her again;
I said, "I love you, Mom."
"I love you too," she said.
Oh, there are volumes,
Volumes of words
That never get said;
But in that situation,
Essentials were conveyed.

Oh, my heart bled.
I knew I had to move,
Had to let go her hand,
Had to get up and leave,
Had to leave that room,
Drive my Dad home;
But she'd be alone.
"Wait, I'm coming along,"
She leaned forward and said.

Again it was Mairead,
With her cool loving head
Who quick-thinking said
"We can't leave her like this.
I'll go get the nurse."
The nurse understood;
Came in and told Mom,
"I always cry too
When my boys go home."

My tears were free-flowing,
My heart felt clean broken.
I finally stood up,
Leaned in to kiss Mom,
And we both said "Goodbye."
As we were leaving the room,
The nurse was talking to Mom,

Helpfully distracting her
From this painful departure.

Tears were blinding my eyes,
I was moving in slow motion;
But I had the clear notion
That I wanted one last look.
I did turn my head
And her image is riveted
Forever on my retina:
My last image of my Mom,
My strong vulnerable Mom.

She was sitting in that chair.
We left her there,
And then we were gone.
She always cried
When we parted;
It made leaving harder,
But also showed the bond,
The underlying connection
That underlay the leaving:

Self-sacrificing love,
Which knew I had to go
If I was ever to grow,
To become my own person;
But acknowledged the connection
In the tearful letting go.
That non-possessive love
Which I think is a reflection
Of divine love's launching.

Perhaps one could say
That every parting heralds death,
But is required for life,
For inner potential to grow.
One's inner potential

Can only blossom
With lots of loving blessing
To overcome the terror
Of being on one's own.

The blessing of being believed in
But also of believing
That, because of the Spirit,
One is never actually alone.
There's many a distraction
From feeling grief and pain.
Jesus wept in pain,[186]
And in the gospel of John
Teaches how to move on.

At one point I noticed
How many words he devoted
To tenderly preparing
His frightened disciples
For his death impending.
His physical departure
Would allow Spirit to enter.[187]
The primary image
Is translated "Helper."[188]

That shift from outer to inner
Counteracts the winter frost
Of a loved one's loss.
From in a mother's body-home
We're thrust out and born:
First taste of what's to come:
Being more on one's own;
Yet totally dependent
For life on Someone.

---

186. The Holy Bible (RSV), John 11:35.
187. Op.cit., John 14–16.
188. Op.cit., John 16:7, see footnote "q."

So Mom has gone home.
She didn't die alone.
Two weeks after I left,
She entered final rest.
My brother Dean
And Gayle came
From Denver to stay
With Dad at his home;
They visited Mom daily.

For days she lived on—
Ate nothing nor drank—
Till final day nine.
Other brother Ken
And his wife Pat
Were there that day
With Dean, Gayle, and Dad.
Frighteningly withered,
Her skin was turning black.

The nurse said it'll be soon;
They all entered the room.
She'd been unresponsive,
Shallowly breathing.
It was very hard to see her
Emaciating like that.
While they were waiting
She suddenly cried out,
Then breathed her last.

It had been a sharp cry,
My brothers too remarked it.
When telling me this,
Himself somewhat breathless,
With an emotional gasp,
In wonderment Dad said,
"She saw the angels

Coming to get her."
I'd had the same thought.

Parts of her I've inherited;
They're part of me:
Her emotionality,
Intuitive sensitivity,
Emergent authority,
Searching spirituality,
Prizing of excellency,
Detailed polishing
Of words and wood.

Her weekly letters to me,
Wonderful to receive,
Of hometown events,
New life and deaths,
Maintained contact, yes,
But also, I'd guess,
Helped her process—
Actually memorialize—
Her inner and outer life.

Her last year of life,
She could no longer write;
Couldn't keep things straight,
Which would so frustrate her.
We began to miss her then,
The person she'd been;
But she was determined
To live as fully as she could,
And remember us she did.

Now it's my hands that write.
I began writing poetry
Four years before she died.
She was excited.,
But I also sensed

She was a little envious,
As well she should be,
Having had little opportunity
To fully choose her identity.

But she found her own way,
'Midst life's limitations,
Of giving expression
To the essence of her.
Years and years of letters,
Multicolored afghans,
Partnering with Dad;
Mostly passing along
The faithful love of God.

Hands hands hands.
At our best
We are God's hands,
Doing God's work,
Sharing God's love;
Also in God's image
Being creative;
A sensitive interface
Between God and world.

www.ingramcontent.com/pod-product-compliance
Lightning Source LLC
Chambersburg PA
CBHW072133160426
43197CB00012B/2092